SUBSIDIA BIBLICA

49

Dean P. Béchard

Syntax of New Testament Greek

A Student's Manual

G&BP
Pontificia Università Gregoriana
Pontificio Istituto Biblico

Cover: Serena Aureli
Impaginazione a cura dell'Autore

Gregorian & Biblical Press
Piazza della Pilotta 35, 00187 - Roma
www.gbpress.org - books@biblicum.com

ISBN 978-88-7653-**708**-0

To the students of the Pontifical Biblical Institute,

past, present, and future.

TABLE OF CONTENTS

Abbreviations

ANRW	*Aufstieg und Niedergang der römischen Welt: Geschichte und Kultur Roms im Spiegel der neueren Forschung.* (ed. H. Temporini – W. Haase; Berlin 1972 –)
ASBF	Analecta. Studium Biblicum Franciscanum
BDAG	W. Bauer – F.W. Danker – W.F. Arndt – F.W. Gingrich, *Greek-English Lexicon of the New Testament and Other Early Christian Literature* (Chicago, IL [3]1999)
BDF	F. Blass – A. Debrunner – R.W. Funk, *A Greek Grammar of the New Testament and Other Early Christian Literature* (Chicago, IL 1961)
Bib	*Biblica*
ExpTim	*Expository Times*
GTJ	*Grace Theological Journal*
JSNT.S	Journal for the Study of the New Testament: Supplement Series
LSJ	H.G. Liddell – R. Scott – H.S. Jones, *A Greek-English Lexicon* (Oxford [9]1996)
NovT	*Novum Testamentum*
NTTS	New Testament Tools and Studies
RB	*Revue biblique*

Bibliography of Reference Works

Lexicons

ABBOTT-SMITH, G., *A Manual Greek Lexicon of the New Testament* (Edinburgh 1922)

BAUER, W. – DANKER, F.W. – ARNDT, W.F. – GINGRICH, F.W., *A Greek-English Lexicon of the New Testament and Other Early Christian Literature* (Chicago, IL ^{3}1999)

CHANTRAINE, P., *Dictionnaire étymologique de la language grecque: Histoire des mots*, 4 vols. (Paris 1968-1980, ^{2}1999)

GARCÍA SANTOS, A.A., *Diccionario del Greco Biblico: Setenta y Nuevo Testamento* (Estella [Navarra] 2011)

FRIBERG, B. – FRIBERG, T. – MILLER, N.F., *Analytic Lexicon of the Greek New Testament* (Grand Rapids, MI 2000)

FRISK, H., *Griechisches etymologisches Wörterbuch*, 3 vols. (Heidelberg 1960-1972)

LAMPE, G.W.H., *A Patristic Greek Lexicon* (Oxford 1961)

LIDDELL, H.G. – SCOTT, R., *A Greek-English Lexicon: A New Edition revised and augmented throughout* by H.S. JONES, assisted by R. MCKENZIE (9th ed.; Oxford 1925-1940; repr. 1966; with revised supplement, 1996)

LOUW, J.P. – NIDA, E.A., *Greek-English Lexicon of the New Testament Based on Semantic Domains*, 2 vols. (New York 1989)

MONTANARI, F., *Vocabolario della lingua greca* (Torino ^{2}2004)

MOULTON, J.H. – MILLIGAN, G., *The Vocabulary of the Greek Testament Illustrated from the Papyri and Other Non-Literary Sources* (London ^{2}1957)

ROCCI, L. (et al.), *Vocabolario greco italiano* (Roma 2011)

RUSCONI, C., *Vocabolario del greco del Nuovo Testamento* (Bologna ^{2}1997)

STEPHANUS, H., *Thesaurus Graecae Linguae*, 8 vols. (repr. Graz 1954)

THAYER, J.H., *Greek-English Lexicon* (1886; repr. Peabody, MA 1996)

VAN WINDEKENS, A.J., *Dictionnaire étymologique complémentaire de la langue grecque: Nouvelles contributions à l'interprétation historique e comparée du vocabulaire* (Leuven 1986)

ZORELL, F., *Lexicon Graecum Novi Testamenti* (Paris 1904, ^{3}1961; Rome ^{5}1999)

Grammars

ABEL, F.-M., *Grammaire du Grec biblique, suivie d'un choix de papyrus* (Paris ^{2}1927)

BLASS, F. – DEBRUNNER, A. – FUNK, R.W., *A Greek Grammar of the New Testament and Other Early Christian Literature* (Chicago, IL 1961)

HOFFMANN, E.G. – VON SIEBENTHAL, H., *Griechische Grammatik zum Neuen Testament* (Riehen ^{2}1990)

HUMBERT, J., *Syntaxe grecque* (Paris ^{3}1960)

MOULE, C.F.D., *An Idiom-Book of New Testament Greek* (Cambridge ^{2}1959)

MOULTON, J.H., *A Grammar of New Testament Greek*. Vol. 1, *Prolegomena* (Edinburgh [3]1908)

MOULTON, J.H. – HOWARD, W.F., *A Grammar of New Testament Greek*. Vol. 2, *Accidence and Word Formation* (Edinburgh 1929)

MOULTON, J.H. – TURNER, N., *A Grammar of New Testament Greek*. Vol. 3, *Syntax* (Edinburgh 1963)

MOULTON, J.H. – TURNER, N., *A Grammar of New Testament Greek*. Vol. 4, *Style* (Edinburgh 1976)

PORTER, S.E., *Idioms of the Greek New Testament* (Biblical Languages, Greek; Sheffield [2]1996)

ROBERTSON, A.T., *A Grammar of the Greek New Testament in Light of Historical Research* (New York [4]1923)

SCHWYZER, E., *Griechische Grammatik auf der Grundlage von Karl Brugmanns griechischer Grammatik* (Handbuch der Altertumswissenschaft II/I.1-3; Munich [2]1959)

SMYTH, H.W., *Greek Grammar* (rev. ed. by G.M. MESSING; Cambridge, MA 1956)

WALLACE, D.B., *Greek Grammar Beyond the Basics: An Exegetical Syntax of the New Testament* (Grand Rapids, MI 1996)

YOUNG, R.A., *Intermediate New Testament: A Linguistic and Exegetical Approach* (Nashville, TN 1994)

ZERWICK, M., *Biblical Greek Illustrated by Examples* (trans. J. SMITH; SPIB 114; Rome 1963)

CHAPTER ONE
SYNTAX: GENERAL INTRODUCTION

Select bibliography for further study:[1] ABEL, *Grammaire*, 356-366; BDF §§ 458-478; HOFFMANN – SIEBENTHAL, *Grammatik*, §§ 266-292; HUMBERT, *Syntaxe*, 65-99; MOULTON – TURNER, *Syntax*, 318-323; PORTER, *Idioms*, 286-297; RADERMACHER, L., "Besonderheiten der Koine-Syntax", *Wiener Studien (Zeitschrift für Klassische Philologie)* 31 (1909) 1-12; ROBERTSON, *Grammar*, 390-445; SCHWYZER, *Grammatik*, 5-17, 619-698; SMYTH, *Grammar*, §§ 900-921, 2153-2279, 2369-2768; WALLACE, *Grammar*, 656-665; YOUNG, *Intermediate*, 205-219.

1. GENERAL INTRODUCTION

"Syntax" (σύνταξις) denotes the deliberate arrangement of linguistic elements (words, phrases, clauses) within grammatical relationships. The careful analysis of these syntactical relationships is essential for understanding the meaning conveyed by each linguistic element and by the sentence as a whole.

1.1. Parts of Speech

Each word contributes to the meaning of the sentence by performing a grammatical function that determines the word's relation to other words in the sentence. There are eight different kinds of words, called "parts of

[1] For complete bibliographical information of the sources cited in an abbreviated form, see "Bibliography of Reference Works" on pp. xvii-xix.

speech" (τὰ μέρη τοῦ λόγου), and each type of word performs a basic grammatical function within the syntax of the sentence. The eight "parts of speech" are the following:

Noun: a word that designates a person (e.g., κύριος) or a thing (e.g., λόγος) or a substantivized action (e.g., τὸ λέγειν)

Verb: a word that designates an action or a state of being

Adjective: a word that modifies a noun/pronoun with which it agrees (in gender, number, and case) by attributing to it a quality (ὁ κύριος ὁ <u>ἀγαθός</u>) or an action (ὁ κύριος ὁ <u>λέγων</u>); note that a participle is an adjective derived from a verb

Article: a word that modifies the noun with which it agrees (in gender, number, and case) by pointing to a particular individual (<u>ὁ</u> κύριος, "*the* Lord"), or to a generic class (<u>οἱ</u> ἄνθρωποι, "men"), or to an abstract concept (<u>ἡ</u> ἀρετή, "virtue")

Pronoun: a word that stands in place of a another noun (person or object) that the reader is expected to recognize from the context; pronouns can be personal (αὐτός αὐτή αὐτό), demonstrative (οὗτος αὕτη τοῦτο), relative (ὅς ἥ ὅ), or interrogative (τίς τί)

Preposition: a word used in connection with a noun (usually preceding it) to form a "prepositional phrase", which can function like an adjective (modifying a noun) or like an adverb (limiting the action of the verb)

Adverb: an indeclinable word that modifies or limits the action of the verb

Conjunction: a "linking word" that connects linguistic elements (words, clauses, sentences) in a logically determined relationship

1.2. Phrases

Meaning is conveyed when words are combined in what may be called "sense units" of varying size and complexity. The shortest and simplest sense unit is called a *phrase*, which often includes a preposition and a noun or pronoun:

ἐν ταῖς ἡμέραις ταύταις ("in those days")
κατὰ πόλιν ("in every city")
διὰ τοῦτο ("for this [reason]")
περὶ τῆς βασιλείας τοῦ θεοῦ ("about the Kingdom of God")
εἰς τὸν οὐρανόν ("into heaven")
πρὸς τὴν θάλασσαν ("to the sea")

1.3. Clauses

A *clause* is a larger sense unit which normally contains a subject and a predicate expressed either by a finite form of the verb or by a non-finite verbal form such as a participle or an infinitive. When the action is expressed with a finite form of the verb, the subject (agent) of the action is expressed with a noun or pronoun in the nominative case, or it is indicated implicitly by the form of the verb. While some verbs have an intransitive meaning (not defined by a direct object), most verbs express a transitive action that is further specified by a direct or indirect complement.

ἐδάκρυσεν ὁ Ἰησοῦς "Jesus wept" (John 11,35): intransitive action

τοῦτον τὸν Ἰησοῦν ἀνέστησεν ὁ θεός "This Jesus God raised up" (Acts 2,32): transitive action

A clause can be either *independent* or *dependent*. An independent clause represents a unit of thought that is complete in itself and so can stand alone as a complete sentence (Subject – Verb [– Object]). In contrast, a dependent clause is a unit of thought that cannot stand on its own, but depends on some other element in the sentence. The function of a dependent clause is to modify or complete the meaning of the element on which it depends. When linked with a noun, a dependent clause stands in a *substantival relation* to that noun. When linked with another clause, a dependent clause stands in a *subordinate relation* to that clause.

τὸν δὲ ἀρχηγὸν τῆς ζωῆς ἀπεκτείνατε ὃν ὁ θεὸς ἤγειρεν ἐκ νεκρῶν "You killed the author of life, whom God raised from the dead" (Acts 3,15): substantival

τί με δεῖ ποιεῖν ἵνα σωθῶ; "What must I do in order that I may be saved?" (Acts 16,30): subordinate

τοῦτον ὁ θεὸς ἀρχηγὸν καὶ σωτῆρα ὕψωσεν τῇ δεξιᾷ αὐτοῦ τοῦ δοῦναι μετάνοιαν τῷ Ἰσραὴλ καὶ ἄφεσιν ἁμαρτιῶν "God exalted him at his right hand as leader and savior, to give repentance to Israel and forgiveness of sins" (Acts 5,31): subordinate

2. The Simple Sentence

A simple sentence is a self-standing unit of thought that can take several forms:

Statement: an assertion of a fact in the past, present, or future, with the verb in the indicative mood

Question: an interrogative statement, which is often introduced by an interrogative pronoun, adjective, or adverb

Command: a volitional statement with the verb in the imperative mood to express what the speaker wants others to do (2nd person), or what the speaker wants to happen (3rd person)

Exhortation: a volitional statement with the verb in the subjunctive mood (1st person plural) to exhort others to join the speaker in doing some action

Prohibition: a negative volitional statement (μή + present imperative, or μή + aorist subjunctive) to express what the speaker does not want others to do (2nd person) or what the speaker does not want to happen (3rd person)

Wish: a volitional statement with the verb in the optative mood to express what the speaker hopes or wishes will happen in the future

2.1. Syntax of the Simple Sentence

In each of the forms listed above, the simple sentence expresses a complete unit of thought, which includes a "subject" (the person or thing that acts or is acted upon) and a "predicate" (the principal action expressed by the verb and often further defined by direct and/or indirect complements). There are no fixed rules for how the words in a simple sentence are to be arranged, since the grammatical function of each word is determined, not by its position in the arrangement of the sentence (as in many modern languages), but rather by the form of the word (i.e., its *case*) or by the use of a preposition. In narrative prose, however, it is possible to discern certain tendencies that create something of a "normal word order".

In the "normal" word order, the simple sentence begins with some sort of "connector" that links the sentence with the preceding statement. This is often a simple conjunction, such as καί, δέ, or ἀλλά. In other instances, the simple sentence begins with a prepositional phrase that creates some sort of transition: to establish a link with the preceding statement, or to indicate the logical relevance of what is now affirmed in the statement that follows. Examples of prepositional phrases that serve as introductory transitions include the following:

> ἐν ταύταις δὲ ταῖς ἡμέραις κατῆλθον ἀπὸ Ἱεροσολύμων προφῆται εἰς Ἀντιόχειαν "In these days, prophets came down to Antioch from Jerusalem" (Acts 11,27)
>
> διὰ τοῦτο ἐν παραβολαῖς αὐτοῖς λαλῶ "For this [reason] I speak to them in parables" (Matt 13,13)

<u>ἐκ τούτου</u> πολλοὶ [ἐκ] τῶν μαθητῶν αὐτοῦ ἀπῆλθον εἰς τὰ ὀπίσω καὶ οὐκέτι μετ᾽ αὐτοῦ περιεπάτουν "<u>After this</u> (or "<u>Because of this</u>"), many of his disciples withdrew and no longer went about with him" (John 6,66)

In many simple sentences, the transitional conjunction or phrase stands at the beginning, and then follows the main elements of the statement in the following order: Verb + Subject + Direct/Indirect Complement. It must be noted, however, that this order is never strictly observed. Any element in the sentence can be advanced to the beginning, or delayed until the end, for emphasis.

2.2. Interruptions in the Syntax of the Simple Sentence

Asyndeton: this occurs when an independent clause is not introduced by a conjunctive word or transitional phrase. This stylistic feature is employed for rhetorical effect; it is often found in a series of solemn commands, exhortations or assertions, such as the proclamation of the "Beatitudes" (Luke 6,20b-21):

μακάριοι οἱ πτωχοί, ὅτι ὑμετέρα ἐστὶν ἡ βασιλεία τοῦ θεοῦ.
μακάριοι οἱ πεινῶντες νῦν, ὅτι χορτασθήσεσθε.
μακάριοι οἱ κλαίοντες νῦν, ὅτι γελάσετε.
"Blessed are you poor, for yours is the Kingdom of God.
Blessed are you that hunger now, for you shall be satisfied.
Blessed are you that weep now, for you shall laugh."

Dislocation: this occurs when closely related linguistic elements are broken up in order to give greater emphasis to the elements by their isolation in the sentence.

<u>ἀνθρώπου τινὸς πλουσίου</u> εὐφόρησεν <u>ἡ χώρα</u> "The land of a certain rich man produced abundantly" (Luke 12,16)

ἐπιποθῶ γὰρ ἰδεῖν ὑμᾶς, ἵνα <u>τι</u> μεταδῶ <u>χάρισμα</u> ὑμῖν <u>πνευματικὸν</u> εἰς τὸ στηριχθῆναι ὑμᾶς "I long to see you, so that I may impart to you some spiritual gift to strengthen you" (Rom 1,11)

Parenthesis: this occurs when the syntax of the sentence is suspended in order to allow for the insertion of a parenthetical comment that often explains or amplifies an element mentioned in the sentence.

> καὶ ἐν ταῖς ἡμέραις ταύταις ἀναστὰς Πέτρος ἐν μέσῳ τῶν ἀδελφῶν εἶπεν·
> — ἦν τε ὄχλος ὀνομάτων ἐπὶ τὸ αὐτὸ ὡσεὶ ἑκατὸν εἴκοσι —
> ἄνδρες ἀδελφοί, ἔδει πληρωθῆναι τὴν γραφήν [...]
> "In these days, Peter stood up among the brothers and said:
> — the company of persons was all together about 120 —
> "Brothers, it was necessary that the scripture be fulfilled [...]
> (Acts 1,15-16)

Anacoluthon: this occurs when a linguistic element (word, phrase, or clause) is inserted but does not fit within the syntactical structure of the sentence; while this phenomenon occurs often in spoken language, its occurrence in written composition is open to various explanations: an unintended error by the author, or a device deliberately chosen by the author to heighten rhetorical or dramatic effect.

> πολλοὶ γὰρ τῶν ἐχόντων πνεύματα ἀκάθαρτα βοῶντα φωνῇ μεγάλῃ ἐξήρχοντο "For many of those who had unclean spirits ... the spirits, crying with a loud voice, came out" (Acts 8,7): the grammatical subject of the verb ἐξήρχοντο is πολλοί, but the subject *ad sensum* is πνεύματα

> ἀπὸ δὲ τῶν δοκούντων εἶναί τι ὁποῖοί ποτε ἦσαν οὐδέν μοι διαφέρει· πρόσωπον [ὁ] θεὸς ἀνθρώπου οὐ λαμβάνει ἐμοὶ γὰρ οἱ δοκοῦντες οὐδὲν προσανέθεντο "And from those who were reputed to be something — what they were means nothing to me; God shows no partiality — those of repute added nothing to me" (Gal 2,6)

3. COMPOUND AND COMPLEX SENTENCES

Simple sentences are independent units of thought (subject + predicate), which are called "clauses" when two or more are combined to form a larger sentence. Clauses can be combined in one of two ways: by coordination (*parataxis*) or by subordination (*hypotaxis*). When two or more clauses are linked by a "coordinating conjunction" (e.g., καί), the result is a *compound sentence*: a loosely connected series of complete statements linked together in a coordinating arrangement. In contrast, when a clause is linked to another clause by some form of subordination (e.g., a subordinating conjunction such as ἵνα or ὥστε), the result is a *complex sentence*. In a complex sentence, the subordinated clause cannot stand on its own, but rather depends on the main clause for the meaning it conveys. Therefore, a complex sentence consists of (1) a main (independent) clause and (2) at least one dependent clause linked in some form of subordination. The difference between these two types of syntactical arrangement can be observed in the following examples:

Compound sentence:

> ἦλθεν ὁ Ἰησοῦς καὶ ἔστη εἰς τὸ μέσον καὶ λέγει αὐτοῖς· εἰρήνη ὑμῖν "Jesus came, and he stood among them, and he said: 'Peace be with you'" (John 20,19): three simple sentences linked together by the coordinating conjunction καί

Complex sentence:

> οὐ γὰρ ἀπέστειλεν ὁ θεὸς τὸν υἱὸν εἰς τὸν κόσμον ἵνα κρίνῃ τὸν κόσμον, ἀλλ' ἵνα σωθῇ ὁ κόσμος δι' αὐτοῦ "For God sent the Son into the world, not to condemn the world, but that the world might be saved through him" (John 3,17): main clause followed by dependent clauses that express the purpose of the main action

Both styles of composition — paratactic and hypotactic — can be found in ancient Greek writings. The loose, paratactic arrangement of compound sentences tends to be found in simple narratives where the author is imitating the plain style of the spoken language. In contrast, the elevated style of literary composition is characterized by the use of subordinate clauses in the formation of complex sentences. Few of the NT writings rise to the level of artistically developed prose. The unadorned narrative accounts of the Gospels (esp. Mark) are characterized by a paratactic arrangement of simple and compound sentences. The use of subordinate clauses distinguishes the hypotactic style adopted by the more literary authors — Paul, Luke, and the author of the Letter to the Hebrews. In the highly polished sentence that forms the prologue of his Gospel (1,1-4), Luke demonstrates his capacity to compose in an elevated literary style. Apart from this very formal introduction, however, Luke joins the other NT Evangelists in adopting a relatively plain style of composition suitable for a widely diversified readership.

4. SYNTAX OF COMPOUND SENTENCES

A compound sentence is formed when two or more simple sentences are combined by a coordinating conjunction, and so placed "side-by-side" (*parataxis*). Different types of coordinating conjunctions are used to indicate, more precisely, the logical connection between the clauses that make up a compound sentence. Such logical connections include the following:

Copulative: καί, δέ ("and") used to link or add a further statement to a preceding statement.

Adversative: ἀλλά ("but", for direct contrast), δέ ("but", for general contrast), πλήν ("but in any case"), μέν ... δέ ("on the one hand ... on the other hand") used to place two clauses in a contrastive relationship.

Correlative: καί ... καί ("both ... and"), οὔτε [μήτε] ... οὔτε [μήτε] ("neither ... nor") used to place two clauses in a parallel relationship.

Disjunctive: ἤ ("or"), ἤ ... ἤ ("either ... or") used to identify two clauses as mutually exclusive alternatives.

Inferential: ἄρα ("then"), διό, οὖν ("therefore") used to introduce the logical consequence of the preceding statement(s).

Causal: γάρ ("for") used to introduce a statement that explains the cause or the basis of what was asserted in the preceding clause.

5. SYNTAX OF COMPLEX SENTENCES

A complex sentence is formed when a main clause (i.e., a simple sentence) is combined with a dependent clause by some form of subordination (*hypotaxis*). The dependent clause can be expressed in several different forms:

- A participial clause
- An infinitival clause
- A relative clause, introduced by a relative pronoun (ὅς, ἥ, ὅ), a relative adjective (οἷος, οἷα, οἷο, or ὅσος, ὅση, ὅσο), or a relative adverb (ὅτε, ὅπου)
- A conjunctive clause, introduced by a subordinating conjunction (e.g., εἰ, ἐάν, ἐπεί, ὅτι, ἕως, ἵνα, ὥστε)

In most cases, the dependent clause follows the main clause, but it can also be advanced to an initial position for emphasis. Within the syntactical structure of a complex sentence, a dependent clause functions in one of three ways: substantival, adjectival, or adverbial.

5.1. Substantival Dependent Clauses

In some cases, a dependent clause is substantivized (forming a "noun clause") and so functions in the sentence just like a noun. When substantivized, the dependent clause can serve as the subject or the object of the main verb. The following are examples of a dependent clause functioning as the subject of the main verb:

> δότε κἀμοὶ τὴν ἐξουσίαν ταύτην ἵνα <u>ᾧ ἐὰν ἐπιθῶ τὰς χεῖρας</u> λαμβάνῃ πνεῦμα ἅγιον "Give also to me this power so that

anyone on whom I lay my hands may receive the Holy Spirit" (Acts 8,19)

ὅτι δὲ ἐν νόμῳ οὐδεὶς δικαιοῦται παρὰ τῷ θεῷ [ἐστιν] δῆλον "That no one is justified before God by the Law is evident" (Gal 3,11)

ὁ πιστεύων εἰς αὐτὸν οὐ κρίνεται "The one who believes in him is not judged" (John 3,18)

φοβερὸν [ἐστιν] τὸ ἐμπεσεῖν εἰς χεῖρας θεοῦ ζῶντος "To fall into the hands of the living God [is] a fearful thing" (Heb 10,31)

The dependent clause can also function as the direct object of the main verb, as in the following examples:

ἐπειδὴ φίλος μου παρεγένετο ἐξ ὁδοῦ πρός με καὶ οὐκ ἔχω ὃ παραθήσω αὐτῷ "For a friend of mine has come to me from a journey, and I do not have that which I may offer him" (Luke 11,6)

ὃ ἑώρακεν καὶ ἤκουσεν τοῦτο μαρτυρεῖ "That which he has seen and heard, this he gives witness to" (John 3,32)

βούλομαι οὖν προσεύχεσθαι τοὺς ἄνδρας ἐν παντὶ τόπῳ "I desire then that the men are to pray in every place" (1 Tim 2,8)

After verbs of speaking (or hearing, or knowing), a dependent clause functions as the direct complement of the verb in that it expresses the content of the speaking (hearing, knowing) in the form of "indirect discourse".

ἀκηκόαμεν γὰρ αὐτοῦ λέγοντος ὅτι Ἰησοῦς ὁ Ναζωραῖος οὗτος καταλύσει τὸν τόπον τοῦτον "For we heard him say that this Jesus of Nazareth will destroy this place" (Acts 6,14)

> ἀκούσας δὲ Ἰακὼβ ὄντα σιτία εἰς Αἴγυπτον ἐξαπέστειλεν τοὺς πατέρας ἡμῶν πρῶτον "And Jacob, having heard that there was grain in Egypt, sent our fathers there for the first time" (Acts 7,12)
>
> ἦλθον λέγουσαι καὶ ὀπτασίαν ἀγγέλων ἑωρακέναι, οἳ λέγουσιν αὐτὸν ζῆν "The [women] came saying also that they had seen a vision of angels who said that he was alive" (Luke 24,23)

Similarly, a dependent clause introduced by ὡς (also ἵνα, ὅπως) functions as the direct complement of verbs denoting "to wish, desire, strive", and so expresses the objective desired or intended by the agent of the main verb, as in the following examples:

> θέλω δὲ πάντας ὑμᾶς λαλεῖν γλώσσαις, μᾶλλον δὲ ἵνα προφητεύητε "I want that all of you speak in tongues, but even more that you prophesy" (1 Cor 14,5)
>
> ἀπ' ἐκείνης οὖν τῆς ἡμέρας ἐβουλεύσαντο ἵνα ἀποκτείνωσιν αὐτόν "From that day on, they took counsel [to determine] how they might kill him" (John 11,53)

Finally, after verbs denoting "to fear", a dependent clause, introduced by μή, expresses the "object" that is feared: an undesired occurrence that may happen in the future (μή + verb in the subjunctive), or an actual, undesired occurrence that has happened in the past or that is happening in the present (μή + verb in the indicative).

> φοβούμενοί τε μή που κατὰ τραχεῖς τόπους ἐκπέσωμεν, ἐκ πρύμνης ῥίψαντες ἀγκύρας τέσσαρας ηὔχοντο ἡμέραν γενέσθαι "And fearing that we might somehow run against the rocks, they let out four anchors from the stern and prayed that day would come" (Acts 27,29)
>
> φοβοῦμαι ὑμᾶς μή πως εἰκῇ κεκοπίακα εἰς ὑμᾶς "I fear that I have somehow labored over you in vain" (Gal 4,11)

5.2. Adjectival Dependent Clauses

A dependent clause can also function as an adjective to define or modify another noun to which it is attached. This adjectival use applies to relative clauses (introduced by a relative pronoun), to attributive participles, and to epexegetical (i.e., explanatory) infinitives.

> ὁ θεὸς τῶν πατέρων ἡμῶν ἤγειρεν Ἰησοῦν ὃν ὑμεῖς διεχειρίσασθε κρεμάσαντες ἐπὶ ξύλου "The God of our fathers raised up Jesus, whom you killed by nailing him to a tree" (Acts 5,30)

> οὗτός ἐστιν ὁ λίθος, ὁ ἐξουθενηθεὶς ὑφ' ὑμῶν τῶν οἰκοδόμων, ὁ γενόμενος εἰς κεφαλὴν γωνίας "This is the stone, the one despised by you the builders, that has become the cornerstone" (Acts 4,11)

> τοῦτο γάρ ἐστιν θέλημα τοῦ θεοῦ, ὁ ἁγιασμὸς ὑμῶν, ἀπέχεσθαι ὑμᾶς ἀπὸ τῆς πορνείας "This is the will of God: your sanctification, that you abstain from unchastity" (1 Thess 4,3)

5.3. Adverbial Dependent Clauses

A dependent clause can also function in an adverbial manner to modify the main clause, just as a simple adverb modifies a verb. Adverbial dependent clauses can be expressed with an infinitive, with a circumstantial participle, or with a conjunctive clause (introduced by a subordinating conjunction). It is used to modify the main clause by indicating one of several adverbial relations: temporal circumstances, purpose, result, cause, condition, or comparison.

Temporal circumstances: An adverbial dependent clause that denotes temporal circumstances can be expressed with a participle or with a conjunctive clause introduced by a conjunction that indicates the temporal relation between the action of the dependent clause and the action of the main clause: ὅτε, ὁπότε ("when, while", simultaneous action), ἐπεί, ἐπειδή ("after", prior action), ἕως, μέχρι ("until", subsequent action). In NT writings, the heightened use of temporal clauses may be the result of the influence of Aramaic, which favors temporal clauses introduced by כְּדִי or כַּד.

Purpose: A dependent clause can express the purpose intended by the agent (i.e., the subject) of the main verb. A clause denoting purpose can be formulated in one of three ways: (1) a conjunctive clause introduced by ἵνα or ὅπως with the verb in the subjunctive; (2) an infinitival clause (simple infinitive, or with εἰς or with pleonastic τοῦ); (3) a future (or present) participle.

Result: A dependent clause can express the result or consequence of what is stated in the main clause. It is often introduced by ὥστε ("with the result that") with a finite form of the verb in the indicative, or with the infinitive.

Cause: A dependent clause can express the cause of what is stated in the main clause. It can take the form of a circumstantial participle, or a conjunctive clause introduced by subordinating conjunctions denoting a causal relationship: ὅτι, διότι, ἐπεί, ἐπειδή, ὡς.

Condition: In Conditional Sentences, the protasis, introduced by ἐάν or εἰ, is a dependent clause that expresses a supposed or assumed case ("If A ..."), while the apodosis is the main clause that states the consequence that follows when the condition is fulfilled ("...then B"). For a more extensive discussion of Conditional Sentences, see Chapter Eight.

Comparison: A dependent clause can express the quantitative or qualitative assessment of an action (or state) in relation to a comparable action (or state) expressed in the main clause. The comparative function of the dependent clause is indicated by the subordinate conjunction that introduces it: ὡς ("as") or ὥσπερ, καθώς, καθάπερ ("just as", often coordinated with οὕτως in the main clause).

Chapter Two
Case Usage

Select bibliography for further study: ABEL, *Grammaire*, 165-203; BAUMERT, N., *Der Dativ bei Paulus. Ein syntaktische Studie mit neuen Interpretationen* (Estudios de filología neotestamentaria 7; Córdoba, 2005); BDF §§ 143-202; CIGNELLI, L. – PIERRI, R., *Sintassi di greco biblico (LXX e NT) 1.1. Sintassi del caso. Le concordanze* (ASBF 61; Jerusalem 2003); CRESPO, E., "The Semantic and Syntactical Functions of the Accusative," *In the Footsteps of Raphael Kühner* (eds. A. RIJKSBARON – H.A. MULDER – C. WAKKER; Amsterdam 1986) 99-120; HOFFMANN – SIEBENTHAL, *Grammatik*, §§ 146-182; HUMBERT, *Syntaxe*, 247-297; MOORHOUSE, A.C., "The Role of the Accusative Case," *In the Footsteps of Raphael Kühner* (eds. A. RIJKSBARON – H.A. MULDER – C. WAKKER; Amsterdam 1986) 209-218; MOULE, *Idiom-Book*, 30-47; MOULTON, *Prolegomena*, 57-76; MOULTON – TURNER, *Syntax*, 206-221, 230-251; ROBERTSON, *Grammar*, 446-543; SCHWYZER, *Grammatik*, 52-173; SMYTH, *Grammar*, §§ 1279-1635; WALLACE, *Grammar*, 31-205; WONG, S. SEK-MUK, *The Classification of Semantic Case-Relations in the Pauline Epistles* (Studies in Biblical Greek 9; New York 1997); YOUNG, *Intermediate*, 9-54; ZERWICK, *Biblical Greek*, §§ 25-74.

1. General Introduction

Each Greek noun can be divided into two parts: a *stem* which conveys the basic idea, and an *ending* which indicates further information about *number* (singular, dual, plural), *gender* (masculine, feminine, neuter), and *case* (nominative, genitive, dative, accusative, vocative). These variations in endings are called the *inflection* of the word. The inflection of a noun, adjective (including participles), and pronoun is called its *declension*, while the inflection of a verb is called its *conjugation*.

The case of the noun, indicated by the ending, determines its grammatical relation to the rest of the sentence. Whereas modern English shows grammatical relations by *word order* or by the use of *prepositions*, in Greek it is primarily *inflection* that indicates how words function grammatically within the syntax of the sentence.

Greek nouns have five cases: *nominative*, *genitive*, *dative*, *accusative*, and *vocative*. The case places the noun in one of a possible number of relations to the rest of the words in the sentence. In Indo-European, the language from which both Greek and English developed, there were originally eight cases. Over time, the Greek noun lost the forms of three of the eight original Indo-European cases and redistributed the functions of the three lost cases (viz., *instrumental*, *locative*, and *ablative*) among the remaining five. The syntactical functions of the (lost) *instrumental* and *locative* cases were taken over by the *dative* case, while those of the (lost) *ablative* case were taken over by the *genitive* case. Thus, the Greek genitive and dative cases are *composite* or *mixed cases*.

The Greek cases fall into two main divisions: (1) *Cases of the Subject* are the nominative and the vocative; (2) *Cases of the Predicate* are the accusative and the dative. The genitive case is used to define either the subject or the predicate.

GENERAL SUMMARY OF THE GREEK CASES

NOMINATIVE: denotes either (1) the *subject* of a finite verb, or (2) the *predicate* of a "linking verb" such as εἶναι or γίνεσθαι.

GENITIVE: denotes a relation that can be expressed by "of" (type of belonging), or by "away from/out of" (type of separation).

DATIVE: denotes the *indirect complement* of the verb ("to/for"), or *means/instrument* ("by/with"), or *location* ("on/in/at").

ACCUSATIVE: denotes mainly the *direct complement* of the verb, but also used to express *motion toward*, or *extension of space/time*.

VOCATIVE: denotes the person(s) directly addressed by the speaker.

2. USES OF THE NOMINATIVE CASE

2.1. Subject Nominative: the nominative is the case of the expressed subject of a finite verb. It names the main topic of the sentence, which, semantically, is very similar to the syntactical subject of the action expressed by the main verb.

2.2. Predicate Nominative: in nominal sentences that employ a copulative verb (e.g., εἶναι, γίνεσθαι), the predicate noun is put in the nominative case. A nominal sentence can express a "convertible proposition" (A = B, B = A). In many cases, however, a nominal sentence expresses a "subset proposition", in that the predicate nominative names the larger class to which the subject belongs: e.g., "The word of the cross is foolishness ..." (1 Cor 1,18).

2.3. Pendent Nominative: a noun in the nominative case that is left hanging in suspension (*pendens*), because it names as the main topic a person or thing other than the subject of the verb in the sentence that follows. This is a type of *anacolouthon* (a break in the syntax of the sentence), which is fairly common in Semitic languages.

> ὁ γὰρ Μωσῆς οὗτος, ὃς ἐξήγαγεν ἡμᾶς ἐκ γῆς Αἰγύπτου, οὐκ οἴδαμεν τί γέγονεν αὐτῷ "For this Moses, who led us out of the land of Egypt, we do not know what happened to him" (Acts 7,40)

Similarly, a pendent nominative is used to express a "title" or a "heading", which, syntactically, is not part of the sentence that follows, as in Matt 1,1; Mark 1,1; Rev. 1,1.

2.4. Appositional Nominative: a noun in the nominative with the article is often used in apposition to a vocative, or in place of a vocative.

> καὶ ἔλεγεν, Ἀββα̃, ὁ πατήρ, πάντα δυνατά σοι "And he said, 'Abba, Father, all things are possible to you'" (Mark 14,36; cf. Rom 8,15)

3. USES OF THE GENITIVE CASE

The name "genitive" derives from *casus genitivus* ("case denoting origin"), which is the Latin translation of ἡ γενικὴ πτῶσις ("case denoting class/type"). The most common function of the genitive is to limit (or define) the meaning of nouns, adjectives, and adverbs; less commonly the genitive can limit the meaning of verbs. The Greek genitive is a composite case, in that it includes (1) functions of the *genitive proper*, and (2) functions of the (lost) ablative case.

3.1. Genitive with Nouns (*Adnominal Genitive*)

The most common use of the genitive is to limit (or define) the meaning of the noun on which it depends (*nomen regens*). This grammatical function of the genitive is akin to that of the adjective. The genitive limits the scope of the *nomen regens* by referring it to a particular class or description, or by regarding it as a part of a larger whole.

> **3.1.1. Genitive of Possession**: to define the *nomen regens* by naming its owner or possessor.

πάντα ὑμῶν ἐστιν, ὑμεῖς δὲ χριστοῦ, χριστὸς δὲ θεοῦ "All things are yours, and you are Christ's, and Christ is God's" (1 Cor 3,22-23)

3.1.2. Genitive of Origin (and Relationship): to denote a relationship that defines the *nomen regens* by naming its source/origin, or by naming the person/class to which it belongs.

τὸν φωτισμὸν τοῦ εὐαγγελίου "the light of [from] the Gospel" (2 Cor 4,4)

οἱ υἱοὶ τοῦ αἰῶνος τούτου φρονιμώτεροι ὑπὲρ τοὺς υἱοὺς τοῦ φωτός "the sons of this age are more clever than the sons of light" (Luke 16,8)

3.1.3. Partitive Genitive: used to denote the larger whole of which the *nomen regens* is a part. NT Greek reflects the general tendency to use the prepositions ἐκ and ἀπό with the genitive to make more explicit this partitive function of the genitive.

τινὲς τῶν γραμματέων εἶπον, Οὗτος βλασφημεῖ "Some of the scribes said, 'This man blasphemes'" (Matt 9,3)

3.1.4. Genitive of Quality: used to express an attribute or quality of the *nomen regens*. This function of the genitive comes closest to that of a simple adjective. A similar usage is common in Hebrew, and for this reason the Genitive of Quality is also called the **Hebrew Genitive**.

καὶ πάντες ἐμαρτύρουν αὐτῷ, καὶ ἐθαύμαζον ἐπὶ τοῖς λόγοις τῆς χάριτος τοῖς ἐκπορευομένοις ἐκ τοῦ στόματος αὐτοῦ "And all spoke well of him, and they marveled at the words of grace [the gracious words] that come forth from his mouth" (Luke 4,22)

Ποιήσατε ἑαυτοῖς φίλους ἐκ τοῦ μαμωνᾶ τῆς ἀδικίας "Make for yourselves friends from the mammon of iniquity [from unrighteous mammon]" (Luke 16,9)

3.1.5. Genitive of Content (also called **Epexegetical Genitive** or **Appositional Genitive**): used to specify the content, or to explain the meaning, of the *nomen regens*.

καὶ σημεῖον ἔλαβεν περιτομῆς "And they received the sign of circumcision" (Rom 4,11)

ὁ δοὺς ἡμῖν τὸν ἀρραβῶνα τοῦ πνεύματος "The One who has given us the guarantee of the Spirit" (2 Cor 5,5)

3.1.6. Subjective and Objective Genitive: when the *nomen regens* is a "verbal noun" (expressing a substantivized action), the adjacent noun in the genitive can express either the *subject* or the *object* of the action expressed by the *nomen regens*.

ἡ γὰρ ἀγάπη τοῦ χριστοῦ συνέχει ἡμᾶς "For the love of Christ controls us" (2 Cor 5,14)

τὸ μαρτύριον τῆς συνειδήσεως ἡμῶν "The testimony of our conscience" (2 Cor 1,12)

ἀπεδίδουν τὸ μαρτύριον οἱ ἀπόστολοι τῆς ἀναστάσεως τοῦ κυρίου Ἰησοῦ "The apostles were giving the testimony of [about] the resurrection of the Lord Jesus" (Acts 4,33)

τὸ εὐαγγέλιον τῆς βασιλείας "the good news of [about] the kingdom" (Matt 4,23)

3.2. Genitive with Verbs (*Adverbial Genitive*)

When not dependent on a *nomen regens*, a noun in the genitive may function either as the immediate complement of the verb, or as a secondary limitation or specification of the action denoted by the verb. Some of these functions belong to the genitive proper, while others are taken over from the lost ablative case.

3.2.1. Partitive Genitive: to denote the direct complement of the verb when the action affects the object only in part.

- with verbs denoting "to take/receive a share of" (e.g., μεταλαμβάνειν, μετέχειν), the complement in the genitive expresses the portion of the larger whole that is received;
- with verbs denoting "to touch" (e.g., ἅπτεσθαι) or "to seize/take hold of" (e.g, κράτειν, ἐπιλαμβάνεσθαι), the complement in the genitive expresses the part of the person or thing that is touched or grasped;
- with verbs denoting "to aim at/strive/desire" (e.g., ἐπιθύμειν, ὀρέγεσθαι) or "to reach/obtain" (e.g., τυγχάνειν), the complement in the genitive expresses the end that is desired or attained;
- with the verb ἀκούειν the complement in the genitive expresses the person whose words are heard.

3.2.2. Genitive of Fulness: with verbs denoting "to fill" (e.g., πληροῦν, πιμπλάναι), the genitive is used to indicate the material with which someone or something is filled.

> πεπληρώκατε τὴν Ἰερουσαλὴμ <u>τῆς διδαχῆς</u> ὑμῶν "You have filled Jerusalem <u>with your teaching</u>" (Acts 5,28)

3.2.3. Genitive of Price: with verbs denoting "to buy" (e.g., κτᾶσθαι, ἀγοράζειν) or "to sell" (e.g., πωλεῖν, ἀποδίδεσθαι), the genitive is used to express the value/price of the thing purchased.

> <u>τοσούτου</u> τὸ χωρίον ἀπέδοσθε; "Did you sell the field <u>for this much [this amount]?</u>" (Acts 5,8)

3.3. Ablatival Uses of the Genitive

3.3.1. Genitive of Time Within Which: used to indicate the span of time within which an event occurred, occurs, or will occur.

> προσεύχεσθε δὲ ἵνα μὴ γένηται ἡ φυγὴ ὑμῶν <u>χειμῶνος</u>, μηδὲ σαββάτῳ "Pray that your flight may not happen <u>during the winter</u>, or on the Sabbath" (Matt 24,20)

3.3.2. Genitive of Comparison: in addition to the construction with ἤ, a comparison can be expressed by the genitive of the person or thing being compared.

> περισσότερον αὐτῶν πάντων ἐκοπίασα "I toiled more than all of them" (1 Cor 15,10)

3.4. The Genitive Absolute

To describe a circumstance involving a person or thing *not otherwise connected grammatically with the rest of the sentence*, a phrase consisting of a noun or pronoun (and any modifiers) plus an anarthrous participle can be put in the genitive case. This usage is called the *genitive absolute.* The term "absolute" indicates that the noun or pronoun in the genitive absolute has *no direct grammatical relationship* to any other word in the sentence. The gentive absolute is usually placed at the beginning of a sentence.

Like other circumstantial participles, the genitive absolute can have a *temporal*, *causal*, or *concessive* relation to the main verb. Adverbs or other words accompanying either the participle or the main verb can make this relationship clearer. Context will help to determine the intended meaning, as in the following examples:

> κρατοῦντος δὲ αὐτοῦ τὸν Πέτρον καὶ τὸν Ἰωάννην, συνέδραμεν πᾶς ὁ λαὸς πρὸς αὐτούς
> "While he clung to Peter and John (*temporal circumstance*), all the people ran together to them" (Acts 3,11)

> γενομένης δὲ τῆς φωνῆς ταύτης, συνῆλθεν τὸ πλῆθος
> "And because this sound occurred (*causal circumstance*), the crowd gathered" (Acts 2,6a)

In Hellenistic Greek (including that of the NT), the genitive absolute is often "misused" in stating a circumstance that does have a *grammatical relationship* with another word in the sentence. This occurs when the noun or pronoun of the genitive absolute reappears as the subject or object of the main verb of the sentence. Examples of this anomalous use of the genitive absolute include the following:

λαλούντων δὲ αὐτῶν πρὸς τὸν λαόν, ἐπέστησαν αὐτοῖς οἱ ἱερεῖς, "As they were speaking to the people, the priests came upon them" (Acts 4,1)

ταῦτα αὐτοῦ λαλοῦντος πολλοὶ ἐπίστευσαν εἰς αὐτόν
"As he spoke these things, many believed in him" (John 8,30)

4. USES OF THE DATIVE CASE

The name "dative" derives from *casus dativus* (ἡ δοτικὴ πτῶσις) because of the common use of the Dative of Indirect Complement with the verb διδόναι. The dative, like the accusative, is an *adverbial* case in that its primary function is to limit or specify the action expressed by the verb or by the sentence as a whole. The Greek dative, however, is a composite case, since it assumes also the functions of two lost cases. For this reason, the dative has three basic functions: (1) to denote the *indirect complement* of the verb; (2) to express *how* the action is done (*instrumental*); (3) to express *where* and/or *when* the action is done (*locative*).

4.1. Proper Uses of the Dative

The primary function of the (proper) dative is to indicate the person or thing indirectly affected by the action expressed in the verb or in the sentence as a whole.

4.1.1. Dative of Indirect Complement: to denote the person or thing indirectly or remotely affected by the action of the verb.

τὰ κτήματα καὶ τὰς ὑπάρξεις ἐπίπρασκον, καὶ διεμέριζον αὐτὰ πᾶσιν "And they sold their possessions and goods, and distributed them to all" (Acts 2,45)

4.1.2. Dative of Interest: to denote the person or thing whose interest is affected by the action described in the sentence; when the person or thing is benefited it is called a **Dative of Advantage**, and when the person or thing is harmed it is called a **Dative of Disadvantage**.

καὶ πάντες ἐμαρτύρουν αὐτῷ, καὶ ἐθαύμαζον ἐπὶ τοῖς λόγοις τῆς χάριτος "And all spoke well about him, and they marveled at his gracious words" (Luke 4,22)

μαρτυρεῖτε ἑαυτοῖς ὅτι υἱοί ἐστε τῶν φονευσάντων τοὺς προφήτας "You give witness against yourselves, that you are sons of those who murdered the prophets" (Matt 23,31)

4.1.3. Dative of Possession: to denote the possessor of something that is said to exist in sentences that employ a form of εἶναι, γίνεσθαι, ὑπάρχειν, etc.; the *genitive of possession* emphasizes the possessor, while the *dative of possession* places the emphasis on the object possessed.

εἶπεν δὲ Πέτρος, Ἀργύριον καὶ χρυσίον οὐχ ὑπάρχει μοι "And Peter said, 'Silver and gold I do not have [lit., are not to me]'" (Acts 3,6)

4.1.4. Dative of Direct Complement with Certain Verbs: to denote the person or thing directly affected by the action of certain verbs, such as: "to follow" (ἀκολουθεῖν), "to draw near" (ἐγγίζειν), "to join, have fellowship with" (κολλᾶσθαι), "to converse with" (ὁμιλεῖν, διαλέγεσθαι, διαλλάσσεσθαι), "to be like" (ὁμοιοῦν); as a general rule, the direct complement of compound verbs is expressed in the dative.

4.2. Instrumental Dative

4.2.1. Dative of Means: to denote the means or the instrument by which an action is done.

καὶ συνάξει τὸν σῖτον αὐτοῦ εἰς τὴν ἀποθήκην, τὸ δὲ ἄχυρον κατακαύσει πυρὶ ἀσβέστῳ "He will gather the wheat into the barn, but the chaff he will burn with an unquenchable fire" (Matt 3,12)

4.2.2. Dative of Manner: to denote the way (manner) in which an action takes place or a state of being exists.

πᾶσα δὲ γυνὴ προσευχομένη ἢ προφητεύουσα ἀκατα-καλύπτῳ τῇ κεφαλῇ καταισχύνει τὴν κεφαλὴν ἑαυτῆς "Every woman who prays or prophesies with her head unveiled dishonors her head" (1 Cor 11,5)

4.2.3. Dative of Cause: to denote the cause or reason for an action or a state of being.

τῇ ἀπιστίᾳ ἐξεκλάσθησαν, σὺ δὲ τῇ πίστει ἕστηκας "They were excluded because of their unbelief, but you have stood firm because of your faith" (Rom 11,20)

4.2.4. Dative of Respect: to denote the respect in which something is true (cf. the "Accusative of Respect" preferred in Classical Greek).

Μακάριοι οἱ πτωχοὶ τῷ πνεύματι "Blessed are the poor in spirit" (Matt 5,3)

γυνὴ δέ τις ὀνόματι Μάρθα ὑπεδέξατο αὐτὸν εἰς τὸν οἶκον αὐτῆς "A certain woman, Martha by name, welcomed him into her home" (Luke 10,38)

4.3. Locative Dative

4.3.1. Dative of Place Where: to denote the place in which something is done; in the NT this is more commonly expressed with ἐν + dative.

τοῦτον ὁ θεὸς ἀρχηγὸν καὶ σωτῆρα ὕψωσεν τῇ δεξιᾷ αὐτοῦ "God exalted him at his right hand as leader and savior" (Acts 5,31)

4.3.2. Dative of Time When: to denote the point of time at which an event occurs.

καὶ ὅτι ἐτάφη· καὶ ὅτι ἐγήγερται τῇ τρίτῃ ἡμέρᾳ κατὰ τὰς γραφάς " [...] and that he was buried, and that he was raised on the third day, according to the scriptures" (1 Cor 15,4)

5. USES OF THE ACCUSATIVE CASE

The accusative derives its name from *casus accusativus*, a questionable Latin translation of the Greek term ἡ αἰτιατικὴ πτῶσις, which is better rendered as *casus effectivus*. The accusative is an adverbial case in that its primary function is to limit the effect of the action of the verb by specifying its extent (or scope), its direction, or its goal. It is the case of the *direct complement* of the verb, i.e., the person or thing affected most *immediately* (in contrast with the dative complement) and most *completely* (in contrast with the genitive complement) by the action of the verb.

5.1. Accusative of Direct Complement: to denote the *direct object* of the verb, i.e., to limit to an *external object* (a person or thing) the effect of the action expressed by the verb.

ἐκπορεύσονται οἱ τὰ ἀγαθὰ ποιήσαντες εἰς ἀνάστασιν ζωῆς· οἱ δὲ τὰ φαῦλα πράξαντες εἰς ἀνάστασιν κρίσεως "They will come forth, those who have done good things to the resurrection of life, and those who have done evil things to the resurrection of judgment" (John 5,29)

5.2. Cognate Accusative: to limit to an *internal object* the effect of the action expressed by the verb; in these cases, the noun in the accusative will be formally or semantically related to the verb (cf. the use of the "Absolute Infinitive" in Hebrew).

ἰδόντες δὲ τὸν ἀστέρα, ἐχάρησαν χαρὰν μεγάλην σφόδρα "Upon seeing the star, they rejoiced greatly with a great joy" (Matt 2,10)

καὶ ἐφοβήθησαν φόβον μέγαν, καὶ ἔλεγον πρὸς ἀλλήλους, Τίς ἄρα οὗτός ἐστιν "And they feared with a great fear, and said to one another, 'Who then is this?'" (Mark 4,41)

5.3. Double Accusative: used with certain verbs to denote two external objects that are involved in the action: 1) the person affected by the action; and 2) the object of the action.

ἐκεῖνος ὑμᾶς διδάξει πάντα "That one will teach you all things" (John 14,26)

γάλα ὑμᾶς ἐπότισα, καὶ οὐ βρῶμα "I gave you milk to drink, not solid food" (1 Cor 3,2)

When verbs that take a "double accusative" are put in the passive voice, the accusative naming the object of the verbal action is preserved, and it is called a **Retained Accusative**.

οὗτος ἦν κατηχημένος τὴν ὁδὸν τοῦ κυρίου "He has been taught the way of the Lord" (Acts 18,25)

καὶ πάντες ἓν πνεῦμα ἐποτίσθημεν "All of us were given one Spirit to drink" (1 Cor 12,13)

5.4. Accusative of Respect (Adverbial Accusative): to limit or define the respect in which something exists or is true.

ἀνέπεσον οὖν οἱ ἄνδρες τὸν ἀριθμὸν ὡσεὶ πεντακισχίλιοι "The men reclined, about 5,000 in number" (John 6,10)

5.5. Accusative of Extent: to indicate the extent of space (how far?) or the extent of time (how long?) in which the action of the verb takes place.

δύο ἐξ αὐτῶν ἦσαν πορευόμενοι ἐν αὐτῇ τῇ ἡμέρᾳ εἰς κώμην ἀπέχουσαν σταδίους ἑξήκοντα ἀπὸ Ἰερουσαλήμ, ᾗ ὄνομα Ἐμμαούς "Two of them were going that very day to a village named Emmaus, sixty stadia distant from Jerusalem" (Luke 24,13)

καὶ ἐκεῖ ἔμειναν οὐ πολλὰς ἡμέρας "And they stayed there for not many days" (John 2,12)

Chapter Three
Verbal Tenses and Moods

Select bibliography for further study: ABEL, *Grammaire*, 249-268; BDF §§ 319-337, 340-356, 357-387; CAMPBELL, C.R., *Verbal Aspect, the Indicative Mood, and Narrative* (Studies in Biblical Greek 13; New York 2007); IDEM, *Verbal Aspect and Non-Indicative Verbs. Further Soundings in the Greek of the New Testament* (Studies in Biblical Greek 15; New York 2008); DECKER, R.J., *Temporal Deixis of the Greek Verb in the Gospel of Mark with Reference to Verbal Aspect* (Studies in Biblical Greek 10; New York 2001); FANNING, B.M., *Verbal Aspect in New Testament Greek* (Oxford 1990); FANTIN, J.D., *The Greek Imperative Mood in the New Testament. A Cognitive and Communicative Approach* (Studies in Biblical Greek 12; New York 2011); GOODWIN, W.W., *Syntax of the Moods and Tenses of the Greek Verb* (Boston 1890); HOFFMANN – SIEBENTHAL, *Grammatik*, §§ 192-212; HUFFMAN, D.S., *Verbal Aspect Theory and Prohibitions in the Greek New Testament* (Studies in Biblical Greek 16; New York 2014); HUMBERT, *Syntaxe*, 110-246; MCKAY, K.L., *A New Syntax of the Verb in New Testament Greek. An Aspectual Approach* (Studies in Biblical Greek 5; New York 1994); MOULE, *Idiom-Book*, 5-19, 20-23, 135-137; MOULTON, *Prolegomena*, 108-201; MOULTON – TURNER, *Syntax*, 60-89, 90-117, 118-133; PORTER, *Idioms*, 20-61, 220-229; IDEM, *Verbal Aspect in the Greek of the New Testament, with Reference to Tense and Mood* (Studies in Biblical Greek 1; New York 1989); RICO, C., "L'aspect verbal dans le Nouveau Testament. Vers une définition", *RB* 112 (2005) 385-416; ROBERTSON, *Grammar*, 821-1049; SCHWYZER, *Grammatik*, 246-354; SMYTH, *Grammar*, §§ 1759-1849, 1850-1965; WALLACE, *Grammar*, 442-586, 713-725; YOUNG, *Intermediate*, 105-146; ZERWICK, *Biblical Greek* §§ 240-291, 295-358.

1. GENERAL INTRODUCTION

1.1. Verbal Moods

The Greek verb is conjugated in four distinct moods: Indicative, Subjunctive, Optative, and Imperative. By the choice of mood, the speaker presents a verbal action/state as an actuality or a potentiality. The Indicative Mood is the *mood of assertion*, which the speaker uses to portray a verbal action/state as a certainty [2]. In contrast, the oblique moods are used to portray the uncertainty of a verbal action/state: as a probability (Subjunctive), as a possibility (Optative), as something intended and/or desired (Imperative).

1.2. Verbal Tenses

In the Indicative Mood, the Greek verb is conjugated in six tenses:

Present
Future
Aorist (from ἀόριστος χρόνος, "undefined time")
Imperfect (from *imperfectus*, "unfinished" or "incomplete")
Perfect (from *perfectus*, "finished" or "complete")
Pluperfect

The *primary* function of each tense is to express the manner in which the action is viewed by the speaker. Only in the Indicative Mood does the tense also designate the *time* of an action as *present*, *past*, or *future*.

Verbal Aspect refers to the way in which an action is viewed by the speaker:

- as an action in progress;
- as a simple occurrence;
- as the ongoing result of a completed action in the past.

---

[2] It is not accurate to identify the Indicative as the mood of fact or reality, since it can be used legitimately in false statements and in fictional accounts, such as parables.

In the Greek verbal system, it is the tense that indicates how the action is being viewed (i.e., the *aspect* of the action expressed by the verb).

- Present tense: for a present action in progress (*progressive aspect)*
- Imperfect tense: for a past action in progress (*progressive aspect*)
- Future tense: for a future occurrence (*aspect undefined*)
- Aorist tense: for a simple occurrence (*simple aspect*)
- Perfect tense: for a present state/condition resulting from a completed action in the past (*completed aspect*)
- Pluperfect tense: for a past state/condition resulting from a completed action earlier in the past (*completed aspect*)

Of course, the choice of tense is made not in the abstract but as part of a concrete utterance and within a specific communicative context. The meaning of the verbal tense, therefore, can often be affected by linguistic factors, such as the lexical meaning of the verb, the grammatical construction in which the verb is used, and other contextual indications. Such linguistic factors must be considered in determining the "affected" (or "contextualized") meaning of the tense of a specific verbal form.

1.3. *Absolute and Relative Time*

The tenses are divided into *primary* tenses (Present, Future, Perfect), which denote present and future time, and *secondary* tenses (Imperfect, Pluperfect, and Aorist), which denote past time. In speaking of the time denoted by the tense of a verb, we must distinguish between *absolute time* and *relative time*. The tense of the main verb of a sentence in the indicative mood denotes an action that is viewed *absolutely*, i.e., it is viewed within the speaker's time frame (at the time of speaking). Consider the following examples:

ὁ θεὸς σῴζει "God saves"
ὁ θεὸς ἔσωσεν "God saved"
ὁ θεὸς σώσει "God will save"

In the first example, the present tense indicates that the act of saving occurs at the current time when the statement is made. In the second example, the aorist tense indicates that the act of saving occurred at a prior time before the statement is made. And in the third example, the future tense indicates that the act of saving will occur at a later time after the statement is made. In the case of all infinitives and participles, on the other hand, the tense indicates *relative time* (i.e., relative to the absolute time of the action expressed by the main verb): the present tense of the infinitive and participle denotes an action that is *simultaneous* to the action of the main verb; the aorist tense (commonly) indicates an action *prior* to that of the main verb; the future indicates an action *subsequent* to that of the main verb. Consider the following examples:

λέγουσιν τὸν θεὸν σῴζειν "They say that God saves"
λέγουσιν τὸν θεὸν σῶσαι "They say that God saved"
ἔλεγον τὸν θεὸν σῴζειν "They said that God was saving"
ἔλεγον τὸν θεὸν σῶσαι "They said that God had saved"

2. TENSES IN THE INDICATIVE MOOD

2.1. The Present Tense

2.1.1. General Use: to denote a present action that is viewed as being in progress (*progressive aspect*), or as something that occurs repeatedly (*repeated aspect*).

2.1.2. Historical Present: the Present Indicative can replace the Aorist Indicative in a vivid narrative in which the narrator presents himself as an eyewitness.

τῇ ἐπαύριον βλέπει τὸν Ἰησοῦν ἐρχόμενον πρὸς αὐτόν, καὶ λέγει, Ἴδε ὁ ἀμνὸς τοῦ θεοῦ, ὁ αἴρων τὴν ἁμαρτίαν τοῦ κόσμου "The next day, he saw Jesus coming toward him, and said, 'Behold, the lamb of God who takes away the sin of the world'" (John 1,29)

2.1.3. Futuristic Present: in confident assertions about the future (e.g., prophecies), the Present is often used to denote a future action, apparently owing to the influence of Aramaic which regularly uses the (present) participle for the proximate future. Ordinarily some temporal indication of the future is included in the sentence.

> καὶ ὑμεῖς οὖν γίνεσθε ἕτοιμοι· ὅτι ᾗ ὥρᾳ οὐ δοκεῖτε ὁ υἱὸς τοῦ ἀνθρώπου ἔρχεται "You also be ready, for at an unexpected hour the Son of man will come" (Luke 12,40)

2.1.4. Gnomic Present: the Present Indicative can be used in a general maxim regarding a timeless truth.

> τὸ πνεῦμα ὅπου θέλει πνεῖ καὶ τὴν φωνὴν αὐτοῦ ἀκούεις, ἀλλ' οὐκ οἶδας πόθεν ἔρχεται καὶ ποῦ ὑπάγει "The wind blows where it wills, and you hear its sound, but you do not know whence it comes and whither it goes" (John 3,8)

2.2. The Future Tense

2.2.1. General Use: the Future is the only tense that indicates only the *time* of the action, leaving the verbal aspect unspecified.

2.2.2. Modal Uses: the Future Indicative can also be used in place of the Subjunctive or Imperative for volitive expressions (i.e., of intention, deliberation, or demand). While also attested in Classical Greek, the noticeable frequency of such modal uses of the Future Indicative in the NT may be attributed to the influence of the legal language of the OT, in which the future is commonly used as a *Categorical Imperative* (e.g., "You shall not steal").

> ἰδόντες δὲ οἱ περὶ αὐτὸν τὸ ἐσόμενον εἶπον αὐτῷ, Κύριε, εἰ πατάξομεν ἐν μαχαίρᾳ; "When those about him saw what was going to happen, they said, 'Lord, are we to strike with the sword?'" (Luke 22,49): Future Indicative in place of the Subjunctive in a deliberative question

ἠκούσατε ὅτι ἐρρέθη, Ἀγαπήσεις τὸν πλησίον σου, καὶ μισήσεις τὸν ἐχθρόν σου "You have heard that it was said, 'You shall love your neighbor and you shall hate your enemy'" (Matt 5,43): Future Indicative with imperatival force

2.3. The Imperfect Tense

2.3.1. General Use: to denote a past action that is viewed as being in progress, or as repeated over a period of time (*progressive/ repeated aspect*).

καὶ λαβὼν τοὺς πέντε ἄρτους καὶ τοὺς δύο ἰχθύας, ἀναβλέψας εἰς τὸν οὐρανό εὐλόγησεν, καὶ κατέκλασεν τοὺς ἄρτους, καὶ ἐδίδου τοῖς μαθηταῖς αὐτοῦ ἵνα παραθῶσιν αὐτοῖς "And taking the five loaves and the two fish he looked up to heaven, and blessed, and broke the loaves, and was giving them to the disciples to set before the people (Mark 6,41)

2.3.2. With verbs of asking and ordering: the very nature of an act of asking or ordering is properly expressed in the Imperfect insofar as the act calls for completion by an answer or by an act of obedience. The incomplete (i.e., "imperfect") aspect of the action is especially prominent when the response is lacking in the narrative.

ὃς ἰδὼν Πέτρον καὶ Ἰωάννην μέλλοντας εἰσιέναι εἰς τὸ ἱερόν, ἠρώτα ἐλεημοσύνην "Seeing Peter and John about to enter the temple, he was asking for alms" (Acts 3,3)

καὶ παρεκάλει αὐτὸν πολλά, ἵνα μὴ αὐτοὺς ἀποστείλῃ ἔξω τῆς χώρας "And he was begging him eagerly to send them out of the country" (Mark 5,10)

2.3.3. With verbs denoting an unsuccessful attempt: the Imperfect is used to present an attempted action that was not carried into effect (*Conative Imperfect*).

> καὶ ἐδίδουν αὐτῷ πιεῖν ἐσμυρνισμένον οἶνον· ὁ δὲ οὐκ ἔλαβεν "And they were trying to give him wine mingled with myrrh to drink, but he did not take it" (Mark 15,23)

2.3.4. With verbs that describe attending circumstances: the Imperfect is often used to describe the action that was in progress when some other action took place.

> ὡς δὲ ἤγγισεν τῇ πύλῃ τῆς πόλεως, καὶ ἰδοὺ ἐξεκομίζετο τεθνηκώς "And when he drew near to the gate of the city, behold, a man who had died was being carried out" (Luke 7,12)

2.4. The Aorist Tense

2.4.1. General Use: to denote a past action that is viewed as a simple occurrence (hence, with "*simple aspect*"). As indicated by the name assigned to this tense (viz., ἀόριστος < α privative + ὅρος, "un-limited" or "un-qualified"), the Aorist presents an action as a simple, unqualified occurrence, without defining the "limitation" (ὅρος) of continuance and/or repetition (expressed by the Imperfect) or of completion (expressed by the Perfect).

2.4.2. Ingressive Aorist: with verbs that express a condition or a state, the Aorist may be used to indicate the entrance into that state or condition.

> γινώσκετε γὰρ τὴν χάριν τοῦ κυρίου ἡμῶν Ἰησοῦ χριστοῦ, ὅτι δι' ὑμᾶς ἐπτώχευσεν, πλούσιος ὤν, ἵνα ὑμεῖς τῇ ἐκείνου πτωχείᾳ πλουτήσητε "For you know the grace of our Lord Jesus Christ, that though he was rich, for your sake he became poor [i.e., he entered into the state of poverty], so that by his poverty you might become rich" (2 Cor 8,9)

2.4.3. Complexive (or Global) Aorist: the Aorist may also be used to designate linear, repeated actions that are regarded as a completed whole. In other words, this use of the Aorist presents as a historical fact a complex of actions that continued over an extended period of time.

> εἶπον οὖν οἱ Ἰουδαῖοι, Τεσσαράκοντα καὶ ἓξ ἔτεσιν ᾠκοδομήθη ὁ ναὸς οὗτος, καὶ σὺ ἐν τρισὶν ἡμέραις ἐγερεῖς αὐτόν; "Then the Jews said, 'This temple was built in 46 years, and you will raise it up in three days?'" (John 2,20)

> τρὶς ἐραβδίσθην, ἅπαξ ἐλιθάσθην, τρὶς ἐναυάγησα, νυχθήμερον ἐν τῷ βυθῷ πεποίηκα "Three times I was beaten with rods, once I was stoned, three times I was shipwrecked, and I was adrift on the sea for a night and a day" (2 Cor 11,25)

2.4.4. Gnomic Aorist: in proverbs or axioms that express a general principle, the Aorist may be used to express an action or state that is valid for all time.

> ἄλλην παραβολὴν παρέθηκεν αὐτοῖς, λέγων, Ὡμοιώθη ἡ βασιλεία τῶν οὐρανῶν ἀνθρώπῳ σπείροντι καλὸν σπέρμα ἐν τῷ ἀγρῷ αὐτοῦ "And he proposed to them another parable, saying, 'The Kingdom of heaven may be compared to a man who sowed good seed in his field'" (Matt 13,24)

2.5. The Perfect and Pluperfect Tenses

2.5.1. General Use: Verb forms in the Perfect conjugation present a completed action that results in a permanent state of affairs (hence, "*completed aspect*"). The Perfect Tense is used to denote a present state of affairs resulting from a completed action in the past, while the Pluperfect Tense is used to denote a past state of affairs resulting from a completed action still further in the past.

> παρηγγείλαμεν ὑμῖν μὴ διδάσκειν ἐπὶ τῷ ὀνόματι τούτῳ, καὶ ἰδοὺ πεπληρώκατε τὴν Ἰερουσαλὴμ τῆς διδαχῆς ὑμῶν "We commanded you not to teach in this name, and behold, you have filled Jerusalem with your teaching" (Acts 5,28)

πτωχὸς δέ τις ἦν ὀνόματι Λάζαρος, ὃς ἐβέβλητο πρὸς τὸν πυλῶνα αὐτοῦ ἡλκωμένος "And there was a certain poor man named Lazarus, who was laid at his gate, full of sores" (Luke 16,20)

ἐτῶν γὰρ ἦν πλειόνων τεσσαράκοντα ὁ ἄνθρωπος ἐφ' ὃν ἐγεγόνει τὸ σημεῖον τοῦτο τῆς ἰάσεως "For the man was more than forty years old, on whom this sign of healing had been performed" (Acts 4,22)

3. TENSES IN THE IMPERATIVE AND SUBJUNCTIVE MOODS

In the Imperative and Subjunctive Moods, the tense of the verb indicates *only* the aspect of the action that is being enjoined or prohibited. In general, the Present Tense is used in reference to *general* precepts concerning attitudes and conduct, whereas the Aorist is used in reference to conduct in *specific* cases [3].

3.1. Commands

The Present Tense of the Imperative is preferred for commands related to general principles that are to be followed (*repeated* aspect), or to ongoing behaviors and/or attitudes that are to be continued (*continuous* aspect). In contrast, the Aorist Tense of the Imperative tends to be used in commands related to a specific action (*simple* aspect). Note the shift from the Aorist to the Present Imperative in what Jesus says to the rich young man:

πάντα ὅσα ἔχεις πώλησον καὶ διάδος πτωχοῖς [...] καὶ δεῦρο ἀκολούθει μοι "Sell all that you have and distribute to the poor [...] and come, follow me" (Luke 18,22)

---

[3] In the NT there are only three isolated uses of the Perfect Imperative: the command, πεφίμωσο ("Be still!") in Mark 4,39, and the formulaic epistolary salutation, ἔρρωσθε ("Farewell") in Acts 15,29; 23,30.

The Aorist Imperative can be also be used for an action that is to be initiated on that specific occasion (*ingressive* aspect), or that is to be repeated over a period of time (*complexive* aspect). The Aorist Imperative is regularly used in greetings and in petitions addressed to God in prayer (*simple* or *complexive* aspect). The difference between the Present and Aorist Imperative can be observed in the Matthean and Lukan formulations of the same *logion*:

χαίρετε καὶ ἀγαλλιᾶσθε,	χάρητε ἐν ἐκείνῃ τῇ ἡμέρᾳ
	καὶ σκιρτήσατε,
ὅτι ὁ μισθὸς ὑμῶν πολὺς	ἰδοὺ γὰρ ὁ μισθὸς ὑμῶν πολὺς
ἐν τοῖς οὐρανοῖς	ἐν τῷ οὐρανῷ
"Rejoice and be glad,	"Rejoice on that day
	and leap for joy,
for your reward is great	for behold, your reward is great
in heaven" (Matt 5,12)	in heaven" (Luke 6,23)

Similarly, in the two slightly different versions of the Lord's Prayer, preserved in Matt 6,9-13 and Luke 11,2-4, the divergent uses of the Present and the Aorist Imperative add different nuances to the petitions expressed in the prayer:

Πάτερ ἡμῶν ὁ ἐν τοῖς οὐρανοῖς·	Πάτερ,
ἁγιασθήτω τὸ ὄνομά σου·	ἁγιασθήτω τὸ ὄνομά σου·
ἐλθέτω ἡ βασιλεία σου·	ἐλθέτω ἡ βασιλεία σου·
γενηθήτω τὸ θέλημά σου	
ὡς ἐν οὐρανῷ καὶ ἐπὶ γῆς·	
τὸν ἄρτον ἡμῶν τὸν ἐπιούσιον	τὸν ἄρτον ἡμῶν τὸν ἐπιούσιον
δὸς ἡμῖν σήμερον·	δίδου ἡμῖν τὸ καθ' ἡμέραν·
καὶ ἄφες ἡμῖν τὰ ὀφειλήματα ἡμῶν	καὶ ἄφες ἡμῖν τὰς ἁμαρτίας ἡμῶν
ὡς καὶ ἡμεῖς ἀφήκαμεν	καὶ γὰρ αὐτοὶ ἀφίομεν
τοῖς ὀφειλέταις ἡμῶν	παντὶ ὀφείλοντι ἡμῖν
καὶ μὴ εἰσενέγκῃς ἡμᾶς	καὶ μὴ εἰσενέγκῃς ἡμᾶς
εἰς πειρασμόν,	εἰς πειρασμόν.
ἀλλὰ ῥῦσαι ἡμᾶς ἀπὸ τοῦ πονηροῦ.	

"Our Father who art in heaven,	Father,
hallowed be thy name;	hallowed be thy name;
thy kingdom come,	thy kingdom come;
thy will be done,	
on earth as it is in heaven;	
give us *this day* our daily bread;	give us *each day* our daily bread;
and forgive us our debts,	and forgive us our sins,
as we also have forgiven our debtors;	for we ourselves forgive every one who is indebted to us;
and lead us not into temptation,	and lead us not into temptation"
but deliver us from evil"	(Luke 11,2-4)
(Matt 6,9-13)	

3.2. Prohibitions

The Present Tense of the Imperative is often used with μή in prohibitions that forbid the further continuation of an action ("Cease to . . ." with *continuous* aspect) [4]. The Aorist Subjunctive with μή is used (in place of the Aorist Imperative) in "absolute" prohibitions that forbid the performance of an action as a whole (*simple* or *complexive* aspect).

> μὴ ποιεῖτε τὸν οἶκον τοῦ πατρός μου οἶκον ἐμπορίου "Cease to make my Father's house a house of trade" (John 2,16)

> μὴ δῶτε τὸ ἅγιον τοῖς κυσίν· μηδὲ βάλητε τοὺς μαργαρίτας ὑμῶν ἔμπροσθεν τῶν χοίρων "Do not [ever] give what is holy to dogs; and do not [ever] throw your pearls before swine" (Matt 7,6)

3.3. Exhortations

Exhortations ("Let us . . .") are expressed with verbs in the Subjunctive Mood in the first person plural. The tense, Present or Aorist, indicates *only* the aspect of the action that is being recommended. The Present Tense is used for ongoing actions that are to be continued

[4] For a critique of this traditional view, see K.L. MCKAY, "Aspect in Imperatival Constructions in New Testament Greek", *NovT* 27 (1985) 201-226.

(*continuous/repeated* aspect), while the Aorist Tense is used for specific actions that are to be performed (*simple* aspect), or initiated (*ingressive* aspect), or adopted as a general practice (*complexive* aspect).

> εἰ ζῶμεν πνεύματι, πνεύματι καὶ στοιχῶμεν "If we live by the Spirit, let us also walk by the Spirit" (Gal 5,25)
>
> ἀγαπητοί, ἀγαπῶμεν ἀλλήλους "Beloved, let us love one another" (1 John 4,7)
>
> οἱ ποιμένες εἶπον πρὸς ἀλλήλους, Διέλθωμεν δὴ ἕως Βηθλέεμ, καὶ ἴδωμεν τὸ ῥῆμα τοῦτο τὸ γεγονός, ὃ ὁ κύριος ἐγνώρισεν ἡμῖν "The shepherds said to one another, 'Let us go across, then, to Bethlehem, and let us see the thing that has happened, which the Lord has made known to us'" (Luke 2,15)

4. TENSES OF THE INFINITIVE

The Present, Aorist, and Perfect Infinitives indicate *only* the manner or aspect of the action as viewed by the speaker: continuous or repeated action (Present), simple or punctiliar action (Aorist), completed action resulting in a permanent state (Perfect).

In contrast, the Future Infinitive, which leaves unspecified the manner or aspect of the action, indicates *only* the *relative time* of the action in reference to the main verb. The action designated by a Future Infinitive is expected to occur, or is said to have occurred, at a time *subsequent to* the main action of the sentence. In the Hellenistic period, the Future Infinitive largely disappeared from the vernacular, and in the NT it is found only in Acts and in Hebrews, where it is used, along with the Present Infinitive, as the compliment of μέλλειν (Acts 11,28; 24,15; 27,10; cf. the present infinitive in Acts 3,3; 20,7), ὀμνύναι (Heb 3,18); and μηνύειν (Acts 23,30).

> ἀναστὰς δὲ εἷς ἐξ αὐτῶν ὀνόματι Ἅγαβος, ἐσήμανεν διὰ τοῦ πνεύματος λιμὸν μέγαν μέλλειν ἔσεσθαι ἐφ' ὅλην τὴν οἰκουμένην "One of them named Agabus stood up and foretold by the Spirit

that there was about to be a great famine over all the world" (Acts 11,28)

ὃς ἰδὼν Πέτρον καὶ Ἰωάννην μέλλοντας εἰσιέναι εἰς τὸ ἱερόν, ἠρώτα ἐλεημοσύνην "Seeing that Peter and John were about to enter into the temple, he asked for alms" (Acts 3,3)

5. TENSES OF THE PARTICIPLE

The tense of the participle, a verbal adjective, indicates primarily the perceived manner or aspect of the action. The temporal relation of the participle with the main verb (i.e., simultaneous, prior, or subsequent) is *not* expressed by the participle in itself, and so must be inferred from the context and subject matter.

5.1. Present Participle

While the Present Participle is often used to denote an action that is contemporaneous with the main verb, it can also be used to express either a prior action (in place of an Imperfect Indicative) or a future action (in place of a Future Indicative).

ὅσοι γὰρ κτήτορες χωρίων ἢ οἰκιῶν ὑπῆρχον, πωλοῦντες ἔφερον τὰς τιμὰς τῶν πιπρασκομένων "All those who were possessors of lands or houses, [first] sold them and [then] brought the proceeds of what was sold" (Acts 4,34): the act of selling must be an antecedent action

καὶ ἀποκριθεὶς ὁ ἄγγελος εἶπεν αὐτῇ, Πνεῦμα ἅγιον ἐπελεύσεται ἐπὶ σέ, καὶ δύναμις ὑψίστου ἐπισκιάσει σοι· διὸ καὶ τὸ γεννώμενον ἅγιον κληθήσεται υἱὸς θεοῦ "The angel answered and said to her, 'The Holy Spirit will come upon you, and the power of the Most High will overshadow you; therefore the child to be born will be called holy, the Son of God'" (Luke 1,35): the birth of the child is evidently a subsequent event

In some cases, the Present Participle denotes a "timeless" action that embraces past present, and future as when Paul names Jesus as τὸν ῥυόμενον ἡμᾶς ἀπὸ τῆς ὀργῆς τῆς ἐρχομένης ("the one who rescues us from the coming wrath", 1 Thess 1,10), or when he refers to God as τὸν δόντα τὸ πνεῦμα αὐτοῦ τὸ ἅγιον εἰς ὑμᾶς ("the one who gives you His Holy Spirit", 1 Thess 4,8).

5.2. The Aorist Participle

While the Aorist Participle often denotes a prior action, it can also be used to express an action that is concomitant with the main verb.

> βουλομένου δὲ αὐτοῦ διελθεῖν εἰς τὴν Ἀχαΐαν, προτρεψάμενοι οἱ ἀδελφοὶ ἔγραψαν τοῖς μαθηταῖς ἀποδέξασθαι αὐτόν "When he wished to cross to Achaia, the brothers, while encouraging [him], wrote to the disciples to welcome him" (Acts 18,27)

5.3. The Future Participle

The Future Participle may be used as the complement of the main verb to express purpose. In the NT it appears but rarely and only in Acts.

> δυναμένου σου ἐπιγνῶναι ὅτι οὐ πλείους εἰσίν μοι ἡμέραι δεκαδύο, ἀφ᾽ ἧς ἀνέβην προσκυνήσων ἐν Ἱερουσαλήμ "You are able to ascertain that it is not more than twelve days since I went up to worship in Jerusalem" (Acts 24,11)

CHAPTER FOUR
SYNTAX OF THE PARTICIPLE

Select bibliography for further study: ABEL, *Grammaire*, 321-330; BARRETT, C.K., "The Imperatival Participle", *ExpTim* 59 (1947-1948)165-166; BDF §§ 339, 411-425; BOYER, J.L., "The Classification of Participles. A Statistical Study", *GTJ* 5 (1984) 163-179; HOFFMANN – SIEBENTHAL, *Grammatik*, §§ 227-240; HUMBERT, *Syntaxe*, 127-132, 169-177; KARLEEN, P. S., *The Syntax of the Participle in the Greek New Testament* (Diss. University of Pennsylvania, 1980); MOULE, *Idiom-Book*, 99-105; MOULTON, *Prolegomena*, 202-232; MOULTON – TURNER, *Syntax*, 150-162; PORTER, *Idioms*, 181-193; ROBERTSON, *Grammar*, 1095-1141; SCHWYZER, *Grammatik*, 384-410; SMYTH, *Grammar*, §§ 2039-2152; WALLACE, *Grammar*, 612-655; YOUNG, *Intermediate*, 147-163; ZERWICK, *Biblical Greek*, §§ 360-377.

1. GENERAL INTRODUCTION

1.1. Definition

Participles are *verbal adjectives*. Their *verbal* nature is shown by the fact that they: (1) are formed on verbal tense stems; (2) have both tense and voice; and (3) can govern direct and indirect objects. Their *adjectival* nature is shown by the fact that they: (1) have gender, number, and case; and (2) can modify and agree with nouns and pronouns.

There are active, middle, and passive participles of the present, future, aorist, and perfect tenses. Each of these tenses and voices has forms of the masculine, feminine, and neuter in all cases and in both numbers.

1.2. Tense and Aspect

The tense of a Greek participle for the most part shows the *aspect* of the action as viewed by the speaker. Often, in context, it is also clear that there is a (relative) temporal relationship between the action expressed by the participle and the action expressed by the main verb.

(1) The *present participle* shows progressive/repeated aspect; its action is often *simultaneous* with that of the main verb.

(2) The *future participle*, like the future indicative, has either simple or progressive/repeated aspect; it always indicates *subsequent* action, and usually expresses intent or purpose; it can be translated by the phrase "about to . . ." or "intending to . . ."

(3) The *aorist* participle has simple aspect; the action of an aorist participle is often *prior* to, sometimes *simultaneous* with, that of the main verb (especially when the main verb is in the aorist).

(4) The *perfect* participle stresses the *completion* of the action.

Although the Greek aorist and perfect participles can often be translated by the same English participle (e.g., "having ____ed"), the Greek aorist participle stresses the *simple performance* of the action, while the Greek perfect participle stresses the *completion* of the action and its enduring effects.

2. MAJOR USES OF THE PARTICIPLE

There are three major uses of the participle in Greek: the *attributive,* the *circumstantial,* and the *supplementary*.

2.1. Attributive Use of the Participle

The *attributive participle* functions like any other adjective: to modify the substantive to which it is attached. It is found in the attributive position: between the article and the noun it modifies, or immediately preceded by the article after the noun it modifies. Such participles agree in gender, number, and case with the word they modify. Participles that modify a noun without the article can also be attributive.

Attributive participles can often be translated by a relative clause.

ὁ πιστεύων ἀνήρ [ὁ ἀνὴρ ὁ πιστεύων]	the believing man
τῷ πιστεύσαντι ἀνδρί [τῷ ἀνδρὶ τῷ πιστεύσαντι]	to the man who believed
τοῦ πιστεύσαντος ἀνδρός [τοῦ ἀνδρὸς τοῦ πιστεύσαντος]	of the man who believed

For each of the participles in the examples given above an adjective could be substituted (e.g., ὁ καλὸς ἀνήρ, "the beautiful man"). The attributive participle, like any adjective, serves to limit the noun with which it agrees.

The attributive participle takes all the constructions which the finite verb takes:

ὁ ἐν τῷ θεῷ πιστεύσας ἀνήρ	the man who believed in God
ὁ ἀνὴρ ὁ ὑπὸ τοῦ θεοῦ σωθείς	the man who was saved by God

As with all adjectives, the attributive participle can be used *substantively* as a noun:

ὁ ἀγαθός αἱ ἀγαθαί	the good man the good women

ὁ πιστεύων	the believing man
αἱ ἐν τῷ θεῷ πιστεύσασαι	the women who believed in God

When the action of the participle is negated, οὐ is used with particular substantives, while μή is used with generic substantives:

οἱ οὐ πιστεύοντες	the (specific) men who do not believe
οἱ μὴ πιστεύοντες	men (in general) who do not believe (i.e., unbelievers)

2.2. Circumstantial Use of the Participle

A *circumstantial participle* is NOT in the attributive position. Such participles agree in gender, number, and case with any noun or pronoun, but most often they agree with the subject of the main (finite) verb of the sentence, and so circumstantial participles are *usually* in the nominative case. A circumstantial participle has an adverbial function, in that it names a further action that is subordinate to the action of the main verb. Compare the use of the attributive participle in sentence (1) below with that of the circumstantial participle in sentence (2).

(1) ὁ πιστεύων ἀνὴρ ὑπὸ τοῦ θεοῦ σῴζεται.
The believing man (the man who believes) is saved by God.

Here, the participle πιστεύων is in the attributive position and serves to point out and identify the (specific) man who is being saved, as would the adjective καλός.

(2) πιστεύων ὁ ἀνὴρ ὑπὸ τοῦ θεοῦ σῴζεται.
Believing, the man is saved by God.

In this sentence, in contrast, the participle is *not* in the attributive position, and therefore it is not serving to identify or point out the man. Instead, it gives the circumstances under which he is saved. A circumstantial participle, then, is the equivalent of an adverbial clause which modifies the action of the main verb. It may indicate simply the *general (attendant) circumstances* in which the main action takes place:

> πιστεύων ὁ ἀνὴρ ὑπὸ τοῦ θεοῦ σῴζεται.
> Believing, the man is saved by God.

When justified by the context, a circumstantial participle may denote a subordinated action that was occurring prior to, or simultaneous with, or subsequent to the main action. In this instance, the circumstantial participle answers the question: *When did the main action occur*?

> πιστεύων ὁ ἀνὴρ ὑπὸ τοῦ θεοῦ σῴζεται.
> When he believes, the man is saved by God.

A circumstantial participle may also denote a subordinate action that caused the main action to occur (looking back), or that was the intended purpose of the main action (looking forward). In this instance, it answers the question: *Why did the main action occur*?

> πιστεύων ὁ ἀνὴρ ὑπὸ τοῦ θεοῦ σῴζεται.
> Because he believes, the man is saved by God.

A further possibility is the use of the circumstantial participle to express the means by which the main action was accomplished, or the way or manner in which the main action was done. In this instance, it answers the question: *How did the main action occur*?

> πιστεύων ὁ ἀνὴρ ὑπὸ τοῦ θεοῦ σῴζεται.
> By believing the man is saved by God.

Finally, the circumstantial participle may denote a subordinate action on which the main action depends, answering the question: *Under what conditions did the main action occur*?

> πιστεύων ὁ ἀνὴρ ὑπὸ τοῦ θεοῦ σῴζεται.
> If he believes, the man is saved by God.

The exact function of a circumstantial participle can be made clear by the use of an adverb or conjunction with the main verb or with the participle.

- A temporal adverb, such as ἔπειτα ("then, thereupon"), accompanying the main verb can indicate that a circumstantial participle is *temporal.*

- The adverb ὅμως ("nevertheless") with the main verb indicates that the circumstantial participle is *concessive* ("although...")

- The particle ὡς with a participle shows that the participle expresses an assertion made by the subject of the main verb, but *not* by the writer of the sentence.

- A circumstantial participle negated with μή *is always conditional* (= protasis of a conditional sentence). Otherwise, circumstantial participles are negated with οὐ.

2.3. Supplementary Use of the Participle

The *supplementary participle* completes the idea of the main verb by specifying a further action either of the subject (when the main verb is passive or intransitive) or of the object (when main verb is transitive).

2.3.1. With Verbs of Emotion

Many verbs denoting emotion, such as χαίρειν, ἀγάλλεσθαι, ὀργίζεσθαι, αἰσχύνεσθαι, take a supplementary participle to complete the meaning. While relatively rare in the NT, a good example of this usage may be found in Acts 16,34:

> καὶ ἠγαλλιᾶτο πανοικὶ πεπιστευκὼς τῷ θεῷ "And with all his household he rejoiced that he had believed in God"

2.3.2. With Verbs of Beginning, Ceasing, and Enduring

Many verbs that denote beginning, ceasing, and enduring take a supplementary participle. The participle is generally in the present tense.

In Classical Greek, the verb ἄρχεσθαι, which in the middle voice means "begin", can take either a supplementary participle or an infinitive, with a difference in meaning. The supplementary participle with this verb states the first of a series of actions: e.g., ἀρξόμεθα τοῦτο ποιοῦντες ("We shall begin *by doing this* [and then we shall do that]"). The infinite with this verb, in contrast, indicates the beginning of a single action: e.g., ἀρξόμεθα τοῦτο ποιεῖν ("We shall begin *to do this*"). In the NT, ἄρχεσθαι is never used with a supplementary participle but only with the infinitive, as in Acts 1,1:

> τὸν μὲν πρῶτον λόγον ἐποιησάμην περὶ πάντων, ὦ Θεόφιλε, ὧν ἤρξατο ὁ Ἰησοῦς ποιεῖν τε καὶ διδάσκειν "In the first book, O Theophilus, I have written about all that Jesus began to do and to teach"

The use of a supplementary participle with παύεσθαι ("to stop, to cease") is fairly common in the NT, as, for example, in Acts 5,42:

> πᾶσάν τε ἡμέραν, ἐν τῷ ἱερῷ καὶ κατ' οἶκον, οὐκ ἐπαύοντο διδάσκοντες καὶ εὐαγγελιζόμενοι Ἰησοῦν τὸν χριστόν "And every day in the temple and at home they did not cease teaching and preaching Jesus as the Christ"

The NT also includes numerous instances in which the supplementary participle is used with verbs that convey the notion of enduring or continuing, such as μένειν, ἐπιμένειν. A good example may be found in the description of Peter's reaction when the absent-minded servant, Rhoda, leaves him at the door (Acts 12,16):

> ὁ δὲ Πέτρος ἐπέμενεν κρούων "But Peter continued knocking"

2.3.3. With Verbs of Perception/Cognition

As in Classical Greek so also in the NT, a supplementary participle can be used to complete the meaning of verbs of perception (e.g., βλέπειν, θεωρεῖν, ὁρᾶν, ἀκούειν, κατανοιεῖν) or of cognition (e.g., γινώσκειν, γνωρίζειν, εἰδέναι, ἐπίστασθαι, εὑρίσκειν, δοκιμάζειν).

With verbs of perception:

> ὅτι ἤκουον εἷς ἕκαστος τῇ ἰδίᾳ διαλέκτῳ λαλούντων αὐτῶν "because each one heard them speaking in his own language" (Acts 2,6)
>
> τὸν δὲ ἄνθρωπον βλέποντες σὺν αὐτοῖς ἑστῶτα τὸν τεθεραπευμένον, οὐδὲν εἶχον ἀντειπεῖν "But seeing the man who had been healed standing beside them, they had nothing to say in opposition" (Acts 4,14)

With verbs of cognition:

> ὁ δὲ Ἰησοῦς εἶπεν, Ἥψατό μού τις· ἐγὼ γὰρ ἔγνων δύναμιν ἐξεληλυθυῖαν ἀπ' ἐμοῦ "But Jesus said, 'Some one touched me; for I perceived power going out from me'" (Luke 8,46)
>
> τότε λέγει· εἰς τὸν οἶκόν μου ἐπιστρέψω ὅθεν ἐξῆλθον· καὶ ἐλθὸν εὑρίσκει τὸν οἶκον σχολάζοντα, σεσαρωμένον, καὶ κεκοσμημένον "Then he says, 'I will return to my house from which I came'. And when he comes, he discovers the house empty, swept, and put in order" (Matt 12,44)

2.3.4. With the Verbs λανθάνειν, φθάνειν, τυγχάνειν

A supplementary participle is often used to complete the meaning of three verbs that denote *being* in some modified way: λανθάνειν, "to be unaware" (i.e., "to escape the notice of"); φθάνειν, "to be first" (i.e., "to anticipate, overtake"); and τυγχάνειν, "to be by chance (i.e., "to happen to be"). With these verbs the participle expresses the main idea, and so it is often represented in translation by the finite verb with an adverbial phrase: e.g., ἐτύχομεν τοῦτο ποιοῦντες, "we happened to be doing this," or "we did this by chance". Use of these verbs is very rare in the NT, confined entirely to Luke, Paul, and Hebrews. The verb τυγχάνειν with the sense "to be by chance" appears only in a textual variant for Luke 10,30 (see mss. A C W). A supplementary participle is used to complete the meaning of λανθάνειν only in Heb 13,2:

> τῆς φιλοξενίας μὴ ἐπιλανθάνεσθε· διὰ ταύτης γὰρ ἔλαθόν τινες ξενίσαντες ἀγγέλους "Do not neglet to show hospitality to strangers, for thereby some were unaware while entertaining angels"

Likewise, a single instance of (προ)φθάνειν with a supplementary participle is found in Matt 17,25:

> καὶ ὅτε εἰσῆλθεν εἰς τὴν οἰκίαν, προέφθασεν αὐτὸν ὁ Ἰησοῦς, λέγων [...] "And when he came home, Jesus was the first in saying [...]"

3. Particular Constructions with the Participle

3.1. Participles in Periphrastic Constructions

A periphrastic conjugation of the verb is formed by combining an anarthrous participle (usually present or perfect) with a finite form of the verb "to be" (εἶναι, ὑπάρχειν, γίνεσθαι). This usage is favored in Hellenistic Greek by the general tendency toward greater expressiveness. In the NT, the periphrastic (present participle + imperfect form of εἶναι) commonly substitutes for an imperfect in order to bring out more effectively the continuous or progressive aspect of the action, as in the following example:

> καὶ ἐπλήρωσεν ὅλον τὸν οἶκον οὗ ἦσαν καθήμενοι "and [the sound] filled the whole house where they were sitting" (Acts 2,2)

3.2. Pleonastic Participles

Participles are sometimes used to express graphically a concurrent or preceding action that is implicit in the main verb. This usage reflects a Semitic mannerism of speech, since such implied action is usually left unexpressed in ordinary Greek. For example, a main verb denoting departure or movement to another place is often linked with a *pleonastic* participle such as ἀναστάς or ἐγερθείς:

> καὶ ἀναστὰς ἠκολούθησεν αὐτῷ "Rising up, he followed him" (Mark 2,14)

> καὶ ἐγερθεὶς ἀπῆλθεν εἰς τὸν οἶκον αὐτοῦ "Rising up, he went to his house" (Matt 9,7)

Semitic influence is even more obvious in the frequent use of pleonastic participles with a main verb that denotes "speaking," "asking," or "responding." The imitation of a common formulaic expression in Hebrew (וַיַּעַן וַיֹּאמֶר) and in Aramaic (עָנֵה וְאָמַר) can be found in the stock formula, ἀποκριθεὶς εἶπεν, which is used in the NT even when the notion of "responding" or "replying" is inappropriate in the context:

> ἐν ἐκείνῳ τῷ καιρῷ ἀποκριθεὶς ὁ Ἰησοῦς εἶπεν "At that time, Jesus answering said [...]" (Matt 11,25): not a response to anything said to him

> καὶ ἀποκριθεὶς ὁ Ἰησοῦς εἶπεν αὐτῇ [sc. the fig tree], Μηκέτι ἐκ σοῦ εἰς τὸν αἰῶνα μηδεὶς καρπὸν φάγοι "Jesus answering said to it, 'Never will anyone eat fruit from you again'" (Mark 11,14): addressed to the unspeaking fig tree

Similarly, the redundant use of λέγων with a main verb (of speaking) to introduce direct discourse may be considered to be the result of Semitic influence. It is commonly found in the LXX in those passages where λέγων renders the use of the Hebrew infinitive לֵאמֹר (with the sense of "saying"), to introduce direct discourse. In the NT, this use of λέγων becomes a stereotyped expression, whose pleonastic character becomes especially evident when λέγων is added to a finite form of λέγειν, as in Luke 7,39:

> ἰδὼν δὲ ὁ Φαρισαῖος ὁ καλέσας αὐτὸν εἶπεν ἐν ἑαυτῷ λέγων [...]
> "Seeing [this] the Pharisee who had invited him said to himself, saying [...]

3.3. Independent Uses of the Participle

In rare instances (mostly in Paul), participles can function independently with an imperatival sense, perhaps under the influence of Semitic idiom. In Rom 12,9-13, for example, a series of exhortations is expressed with ten participles without a finite verb:

> 9 Ἡ ἀγάπη ἀνυπόκριτος. ἀποστυγοῦντες τὸ πονηρόν, κολλώμενοι τῷ ἀγαθῷ τῇ φιλαδελφίᾳ εἰς ἀλλήλους φιλόστοργοι, 10 τῇ φιλαδελφίᾳ εἰς ἀλλήλους φιλόστοργοι, τῇ τιμῇ ἀλλήλους προηγούμενοι, 11 τῇ σπουδῇ μὴ ὀκνηροί, τῷ πνεύματι ζέοντες, τῷ κυρίῳ δουλεύοντες, 12 τῇ ἐλπίδι χαίροντες, τῇ θλίψει ὑπομένοντες τῇ προσευχῇ προσκαρτεροῦντες, 13 ταῖς χρείαις τῶν ἁγίων κοινωνοῦντες, τὴν φιλοξενίαν διώκοντες
> " 9 Let love be genuine, hate what is evil, hold to what is good, 10 love one another with brotherly affection, outdo one another in showing honor, 11 never grow weak in zeal, be fervent in Spirit, serve the Lord, 12 rejoice in your hope, be patient in tribulation, be constant in prayer, 13 contribute to the needs of the saints, practice hospitality"

This string of imperatival participles is then followed by three imperatives in vs. 14: εὐλογεῖτε τοὺς διώκοντας [ὑμᾶς], εὐλογεῖτε καὶ μὴ καταρᾶσθε "Bless those who persecute you, bless and do not curse them".

Similarly, participles are sometimes used in place of finite verbs in the indicative. This occurs most often in the Pauline Letters where Paul begins a sentence with a finite verb and then continues with coordinate participles. Again, this usage suggests the influence of Semitic idiom.

οὐ πάλιν ἑαυτοὺς συνιστάνομεν ὑμῖν ἀλλὰ ἀφορμὴν διδόντες ὑμῖν καυχήματος ὑπὲρ ἡμῶν "We are not commending ourselves to you again but giving you reason to be proud of us" (2 Cor 5,12): διδόντες in place of expected δίδομεν

CHAPTER FIVE
USES OF THE INFINITIVE

Select bibliography for further study: ABEL, *Grammaire*, 300-320; BDF §§ 388-410; BOYER, J.L., "The Classification of Infinitives: A Statistical Study", *GTJ* 6 (1985) 3-27; BURK, D., *Articular Infinitives in the Greek of the New Testament. On the Exegetical Benefit of Grammatical Precision* (New Testament Monographs 14; Sheffield 2006); HOFFMANN – SIEBENTHAL, *Grammatik*, §§ 213-226; HUMBERT, *Syntaxe*, 124-127, 159-169; MCKAY, K.L., *A New Syntax of the Verb in NT Greek: An Aspectual Approach* (New York 1994) 55-60; MOULE, *Idiom-Book*, 126-134; MOULTON, *Prolegomena*, 202-222; MOULTON – TURNER, *Syntax*, 134-149; PORTER, *Idioms*, 194-203; ROBERTSON, *Grammar*, 1051-1095; SCHWYZER, *Grammatik*, 355-383; SMYTH, *Grammar*, §§ 1966-2038; VOTAW, C.W., *The Use of the Infinitive in Biblical Greek* (Chicago, IL 1896); WALLACE, *Grammar*, 587-611; YOUNG, *Intermediate*, 165-177; ZERWICK, *Biblical Greek*, §§ 380-395.

1. GENERAL INTRODUCTION

The infinitive is an indeclinable *verbal noun*, denoting a substantivized action. Like any noun, the infinite has number (singular) and gender (neuter) and case (nominative, genitive, dative, accusative); it can appear with or without the definite article (τό, τοῦ, τῷ). Like any verb, the infinite has tense and voice; it can be modified by an adverb; and it can govern a direct and/or indirect object. It is usually negated with μή not οὐ (like other non-indicative verbal forms). If the subject of the action expressed by the infinitive is different from that of the governing verb, it appears in the accusative. The tense of the infinitive indicates primarily the *aspect* of the action as viewed by the speaker: present (*continuous/ repeated aspect*); aorist (*simple, ingressive,* or *complexive aspect*); perfect (*perfective aspect*). In certain constructions, the tense of the infinitive may also indicate a temporal relationship between the action denoted by the infinitive and the action expressed by the main verb of the sentence.

The uses of the infinitive can be classified according to the semantic function of the infinitive in the sentence where it appears. In *nominal* (or *substantival*) *uses*, the emphasis falls on the nominal character of the infinitive (as a verbal *noun*). In *adverbial uses*, in contrast, it is more the verbal character of the infinitive that receives the emphasis (as a *verbal* noun).

2. Nominal (Substantival) Uses of the Infinitive

As a verbal *noun* denoting a substantivized action, the infinitive can function semantically in the sentence just like any noun.

2.1. Subject of the Main Verb

An infinitive, with or without the definite article, can function as the subject of a finite verb. This includes instances in which the finite verb is a so-called "impersonal verb", such as δεῖ, συμφέρει, ἔξεστιν, or δοκεῖ. A subject infinitive is also used in expressions in which ἐστίν is combined with a predicate adjective, such as δυνατόν ἐστίν ("X is possible") or καλόν ἐστίν ("X is good/pleasing").

> τὸ δὲ ἀνίπτοις χερσὶν φαγεῖν οὐ κοινοῖ τὸν ἄνθρωπον "To eat with unwashed hands does not defile a man" (Matt 15,20)

> τὸ δὲ καθίσαι ἐκ δεξιῶν μου καὶ ἐξ εὐωνύμων μου οὐκ ἔστιν ἐμὸν δοῦναι "To sit at my right and at my left is not mine to give" (Matt 20,23)

ἐμοὶ γὰρ τὸ ζῆν Χριστὸς καὶ τὸ ἀποθανεῖν κέρδος "For me, to live is Christ, and to die is gain" (Phil 1,21)

ἀποκριθεὶς δὲ Πέτρος καὶ οἱ ἀπόστολοι εἶπον, πειθαρχεῖν δεῖ θεῷ μᾶλλον ἢ ἀνθρώποις "Peter and the apostles answering said, 'It is necessary to obey God rather than men'" (Acts 5,29)

καὶ ἐπηρώτησαν αὐτόν, λέγοντες, Εἰ ἔξεστιν τοῖς σάββασιν θεραπεύειν; "And they asked him, saying, 'Is it permissible to heal on the Sabbath?'" (Matt 12,10)

ὁ Πέτρος λέγει τῷ Ἰησοῦ· ῥαββί, καλόν ἐστιν ἡμᾶς ὧδε εἶναι "Peter said to Jesus, 'Master, that we are here is good'" (Mark 9,5).

2.2. Direct Object of the Main Verb

An infinitive, with or without the definite article, can sometimes function as the direct object of a finite verb.

ὥσπερ γὰρ ὁ πατὴρ ἔχει ζωὴν ἐν ἑαυτῷ, οὕτως καὶ τῷ υἱῷ ἔδωκεν ζωὴν ἔχειν ἐν ἑαυτῷ "For just as the Father has life in himself, so He has given to the Son to have life in himself" (John 5,26)

μηδενὶ μηδὲν ὀφείλετε, εἰ μὴ τὸ ἀγαπᾶν ἀλλήλους "You owe nothing to no one, except to love one another" (Rom 13,8)

οὐχ ἁρπαγμὸν ἡγήσατο τὸ εἶναι ἴσα θεῷ "He did not consider being equal to God a thing to be grasped" (Phil 2,6)

2.3. Infinitive with Verbs of Perceiving, Showing, and Saying

The infinitive may be used after verbs of perceiving (e.g., ἀκούειν, θεωρεῖν, βλέπειν, γινώσκειν), showing (e.g., δείκνυσθαι, δηλοῦν), and saying (e.g., λέγειν, λαλεῖν). In such cases, the infinitive may be considered the direct object of the finite verb (of perceiving, showing, or saying) insofar as it expresses the content of the perception or communication. In Hellenistic Greek, verbs of perceiving, showing, and saying more commonly govern a participle (supplementary use) or a noun clause (e.g., ὅτι + finite verb). The alternative construction with the infinitive (+ subject accusative) represents a Classical usage, which is retained in the NT mainly by the "literary" authors (Paul and Luke).

ἤκουσαν τοῦτο αὐτὸν πεποιηκέναι τὸ σημεῖον "They [the crowd] heard that he had done this sign" (John 12,18)

ἀκούω σχίσματα ἐν ὑμῖν ὑπάρχειν "I hear that there are divisions among you" (1 Cor 11,18)

ἐπιδεικνὺς διὰ τῶν γραφῶν εἶναι τὸν χριστὸν Ἰησοῦν "showing through the scriptures that Jesus was the Christ (Acts 18,28)

ἠρώτα τοὺς μαθητὰς αὐτοῦ, λέγων, τίνα με λέγουσιν οἱ ἄνθρωποι εἶναι "He asked his disciples, saying, "Who do men say that I am?"" (Matt 16,13)

2.4. Appositional Infinitive

Like any noun, an infinitive can stand in apposition to another noun. In these cases, the infinitive has a *defining function*: it gives a specific example that defines (or illustrates) the general category named by the related noun.

εἰς τοῦτο γὰρ ὤφθην σοι, προχειρίσασθαί σε ὑπηρέτην καὶ μάρτυρα "For I have appeared to you for this reason, to appoint you as servant and witness" (Acts 26,16)

ὁ ἁγιασμὸς ὑμῶν, ἀπέχεσθαι ὑμᾶς ἀπὸ τῆς πορνείας "Your sanctification, that you abstain from unchastity (1 Thess 4,3)

ἐδίδασκεν τῷ Βαλὰκ βαλεῖν σκάνδαλον ἐνώπιον τῶν υἱῶν Ἰσραὴλ φαγεῖν εἰδωλόθυτα καὶ πορνεῦσαι "[Balaam] taught Balak to put before the sons of Israel a stumbling block, to eat idol meat and to practice immorality" (Rev 2,14)

2.5. Epexegetical Infinitive

An infinitive is said to be *epexegetical* when it is used to *explain* or *qualify* another noun or adjective. Note that an appositional infinitive, in contrast, is used to *define* another noun.

> ἰδοὺ δέδωκα ὑμῖν τὴν ἐξουσίαν τοῦ πατεῖν ἐπάνω ὄφεων καὶ σκορπίων "Behold, I have given you authority to trample upon serpents and scorpions" (Luke 10,19).

> βραδεῖς τῇ καρδίᾳ τοῦ πιστεύειν ἐπὶ πᾶσιν οἷς ἐλάλησαν οἱ προφῆται "Slow in heart to have faith in all the things that the prophets have spoken" (Luke 24,25)

> ἰδὼν ὅτι ἔχει πίστιν τοῦ σωθῆναι "Seeing that he had faith to be healed" (Acts 14,9)

3. ADVERBIAL USES OF THE INFINITIVE

The infinitive can also be used to qualify, in some way, the action expressed by the main verb of the sentence. These uses of the infinitive answer adverbial questions, such as: why? with what result? for what reason? how? when?

3.1. Infinitive of Purpose

The simple (anarthrous) infinitive, or the genitive of the articular infinitive, can be used to express the purpose of the main action of the sentence, especially after verbs meaning "to appoint, present, send", and in the NT also after verbs of motion. This use of the infinitive is equivalent to a final (purpose) clause with ἵνα (or ὅπως) + subjunctive.

> μὴ νομίσητε ὅτι ἦλθον καταλῦσαι τὸν νόμον ἢ τοὺς προφήτας· οὐκ ἦλθον καταλῦσαι ἀλλὰ πληρῶσαι "Do not think that I have come to destroy the law and the prophets; I have come not to destroy but to fulfill [them]" (Matt 5,17)

ἐξῆλθεν ὁ σπείρων τοῦ σπείρειν "The sower went out to sow" (Matt 13,3).

ἐπείνασα γάρ, καὶ ἐδώκατέ μοι φαγεῖν "For I was thirsty, and you gave me to drink" (Matt 25,35)

τοῖς ἀγγέλοις αὐτοῦ ἐντελεῖται περὶ σοῦ, τοῦ διαφυλάξαι σε "He will command his angels for you, to guard you" (Luke 4,10)

ἄνθρωποι δύο ἀνέβησαν εἰς τὸ ἱερὸν προσεύξασθαι "Two men went up to the temple to pray" (Luke 18,10)

The construction with εἰς/πρός + τό + infinitive also expresses purpose.

καὶ παραδώσουσιν αὐτὸν τοῖς ἔθνεσιν εἰς τὸ ἐμπαῖξαι καὶ μαστιγῶσαι καὶ σταυρῶσαι· καὶ τῇ τρίτῃ ἡμέρᾳ ἀναστήσεται "They will hand him over to the Gentiles in order to mock and scourge and crucify [him], and on the third day he will rise up" (Matt 20,19)

προσέχετε τὴν ἐλεημοσύνην ὑμῶν μὴ ποιεῖν ἔμπροσθεν τῶν ἀνθρώπων, πρὸς τὸ θεαθῆναι αὐτοῖς "Beware of practicing your piety before men, in order to be seen by them" (Matt 6,1)

3.2. Infinitive of Result

The infinitive can be used after ὥστε (or sometimes ὡς) to express the intended or actual result of the main action of the sentence. In the NT, the ὥστε is sometimes omitted.

καὶ ἦλθον καὶ ἔπλησαν ἀμφότερα τὰ πλοῖα ὥστε βυθίζεσθαι αὐτά "And they came and filled both boats [with the fish], with the result that they were sinking" (Luke 5,7)

Ἀνανία, διὰ τί ἐπλήρωσεν ὁ Σατανᾶς τὴν καρδίαν σου, ψεύσασθαί σε τὸ πνεῦμα τὸ ἅγιον; "Ananias, why did Satan fill your heart, so that you lied to the Holy Spirit?" (Acts 5,3)

In rare instances, the result of the main action can also be expressed by τοῦ + infinitive, or by εἰς + τό + infinitive. These same constructions can also express purpose. In order to avoid confusion, it is important to recall that the infinitive of purpose places emphasis on the intention of the agent (which may or may not be realized), while the infinitive of result places emphasis on the final outcome of the action (which may or may not have been intended).

> τὰ γὰρ ἀόρατα αὐτοῦ ἀπὸ κτίσεως κόσμου τοῖς ποιήμασιν νοούμενα καθορᾶται [...] εἰς τὸ εἶναι αὐτοὺς ἀναπολογήτους "From the creation of the world, His invisible nature has been perceived in created things [...] with the result that they [unbelievers] are without excuse" (Rom 1,20)

> ἐὰν δὲ ἀποθάνῃ ὁ ἀνήρ, ἐλευθέρα ἐστὶν ἀπὸ τοῦ νόμου, τοῦ μὴ εἶναι αὐτὴν μοιχαλίδα γενομένην ἀνδρὶ ἑτέρῳ "But if her husband dies, then she [his wife] is free from the law, with the result that, if she marries another man, she is not an adulteress" (Rom 7,3)

3.3. Infinitive Expressing Cause

The construction with διά + τό + infinitive is used to indicate the cause or the reason for the action expressed by the main verb of the sentence.

> καὶ διὰ τὸ μὴ ἔχειν ῥίζαν ἐξηράνθη "And because it did not have roots, it dried up" (Mark 4,6)

> οἱ Σαδδουκαῖοι διαπονούμενοι διὰ τὸ διδάσκειν αὐτοὺς τὸν λαόν "The Sadducees were annoyed because they were teaching the people" (Acts 4,1-2)

3.4. Infinitive Expressing Means

The construction with ἐν + τῷ + infinitive can be used to indicate the means by which the action of the main verb of the sentence is accomplished.

ὁ θεὸς τὸν παῖδα αὐτοῦ ἀπέστειλεν αὐτὸν εὐλογοῦντα ὑμᾶς ἐν τῷ ἀποστρέφειν ἕκαστον ἀπὸ τῶν πονηριῶν ὑμῶν "God sent his son to bless you by turning each of you from your sins" (Acts 3,26)

3.5. Infinitive Expressing Temporal Circumstances

The articular infinitive can be used with certain prepositions to form a temporal clause, in which a secondary action (expressed by the infinitive) is set in a temporal relationship with the primary action (expressed by the main verb).

Antecedent action: μετά + τό + (aorist) infinitive ("after . . .")
ἐν + τῷ + (aorist) infinitive ("after ...")

μετὰ δὲ τὸ παραδοθῆναι τὸν Ἰωάννην ἦλθεν ὁ Ἰησοῦς εἰς τὴν Γαλιλαίαν κηρύσσων τὸ εὐαγγέλιον τοῦ θεοῦ "After John was handed over, Jesus came into Galilee preaching the gospel of God" (Mark 1,14)

παρέστησεν ἑαυτὸν ζῶντα μετὰ τὸ παθεῖν αὐτὸν ἐν πολλοῖς τεκμηρίοις "With many proofs He presented himself [to them] alive after he suffered his passion [and death]" (Acts 1,3)

ἐν δὲ τῷ ἄρξασθαί με λαλεῖν, ἐπέπεσεν τὸ πνεῦμα τὸ ἅγιον ἐπ' αὐτούς "After I began to speak, the Holy Spirit fell upon them" (Acts 11,15)

Simultaneous action: ἐν + τῷ + (present) infinitive ("while ...")

καὶ ἐν τῷ σπείρειν αὐτὸν ἃ μὲν ἔπεσεν παρὰ τὴν ὁδόν "And while he was sowing, some [of the seed] fell along the road" (Matt 13,4)

ἐν τῷ εἶναι αὐτοὺς ἐκεῖ, ἐπλήσθησαν αἱ ἡμέραι τοῦ τεκεῖν αὐτήν "While they were there, the time came for her to give birth" (Luke 2,6).

Subsequent action: πρό + τοῦ or πρίν (ἤ) + infinitive ("before ...")

οἶδεν γὰρ ὁ πατὴρ ὑμῶν ὧν χρείαν ἔχετε πρὸ τοῦ ὑμᾶς αἰτῆσαι αὐτόν "Your Father knows what you need before you ask him (Matt 6,8)

πρὶν ἢ δὶς ἀλέκτορα φωνῆσαι τρίς με ἀπαρνήσῃ "Before the cock crows twice, you will deny me three times" (Mark 14,30)

3.6. Infinitive as Complement of the Main Verb

The infinitive can be used to complete the meaning of the governing verb. This comes close to instances where the infinitive functions as the direct object of a finite verb. The difference lies in the fact that *complementary infinitives* are used with a special set of verbs that require an infinitive to complete the verbal idea, such as the following:

1) "to wish" (θέλειν), "to desire" (βούλεσθαι), "to strive" (ζητεῖν)
2) "to avoid" (φυλάσσεσθαι), "to be ashamed" (αἰσχύνεσθαι), "to be afraid" (φοβεῖσθαι)
3) "to ask, request" (δεῖσθαι, ἐρωτᾶν, παρακαλεῖν)
4) "to command, enjoin" (κελεύειν, τάσσειν)
5) "to allow, permit" (ἐᾶν, ἀφιέναι)
6) "to be able" (δύνασθαι), "have power" (ἰσχύειν), "understand [how to]" (ἔχειν)
7) "to be obliged to" (ὀφείλειν), "to be about to" (μέλλειν)

Consider the following examples:

εἰ δὲ θέλεις εἰσελθεῖν εἰς τὴν ζωήν, τήρησον τὰς ἐντολάς "If you want to enter into life, keep the commandments" (Matt 19,17)

Ἰωσήφ, υἱὸς Δαυίδ, μὴ φοβηθῇς παραλαβεῖν Μαριὰμ τὴν γυναῖκά σου "Joseph, son of David, do not fear to take Mary as your wife" (Matt 1,20)

Διδάσκαλε, δέομαί σου ἐπιβλέψαι ἐπὶ τὸν υἱόν μου, ὅτι μονογενής ἐστίν μοι "Teacher, I beg you to look upon my son, for he is my only child" (Luke 9,38)

ἔταξαν ἀναβαίνειν Παῦλον καὶ Βαρνάβαν πρὸς τοὺς ἀποστόλους "They appointed Paul and Barnabas to go up to the apostles" (Acts 15,2)

οὐκ ἴσχυον ἀντιστῆναι τῇ σοφίᾳ καὶ τῷ πνεύματι ᾧ ἐλάλει "They were unable to withstand the wisdom and spirit with which he spoke" (Acts 6,10)

ὃς ἰδὼν Πέτρον καὶ Ἰωάννην μέλλοντας εἰσιέναι εἰς τὸ ἱερόν, ἠρώτα ἐλεημοσύνην λαβεῖν "Seeing Peter and John about to enter the temple, he was asking to receive alms" (Acts 3,3)

CHAPTER SIX
CONJUNCTIONS AND SENTENCE ADVERBS

Select bibliography for further study: ABEL, *Grammaire*, 331-355; BEAL, G.K. – BRENDSEL, D. – ROSS, W.A., *An Interpretive Lexicon of the New Testament Greek. Analysis of Prepositions, Adverbs, Particles, Relative Pronouns, and Conjunctions* (Grand Rapids, MI 2014); BLACK, S., *Sentence Conjunctions in the Gospel of Matthew.* καί, δέ, τότε, γάρ, οὖν and Asyndeton in Narrative Discourse (JSNT.S 216; Sheffield 2002); BDF §§ 438-457; DENNISTON, J.D., *The Greek Particles* (Oxford ^{2}1954); HOFFMANN – SIEBENTHAL, *Grammatik*, §§ 250-252; HUMBERT, *Syntaxe*, 368-442; MOORHOUSE, A.M., *Studies in the Greek Negative* (Oxford 1959); MOULE, *Idiom-Book*, 142-147; MOULTON – TURNER, *Syntax*, 329-341; PORTER, *Idioms*, 204-217; ROBERTSON, *Grammar*, 1142-1193; SCHWYZER, *Grammatik*, 553-590; SMYTH, *Grammar*, §§ 2775-3004; THRALL, M., *Greek Particles in the New Testament* (NTTS 3; Leiden 1962); WALLACE, *Grammar*, 666-678; YOUNG, *Intermediate*, 179-204; ZERWICK, *Biblical Greek*, §§ 400-429, 450-477.

1. GENERAL INTRODUCTION

Under the general heading of "Particles" grammarians include two kinds of words:

1) *Conjunctions*: used to express the interrelation of clauses and sentences;

2) *Sentence Adverbs*: used to mark the modal character of a clause or sentence.

Sentence Adverbs are sometimes called "modal particles" (here "particle" is used in a narrow sense of the word).

While many such words function either as *conjunctions* or as *sentence adverbs*, some very common particles fluctuate in usage, being at times conjunctional, and at other times adverbial:

E.g., καί: "and" (conjunctional)
"even" (adverbial)

γάρ: "for" (conjunctional)
"in fact" (adverbial)

2. CONJUNCTIONS

Conjunctions may be either *coordinating* (i.e., those that connect elements in a sentence that are syntactically equal to each other) or *subordinating* (i.e., those that introduce a dependent clause that serves to modify some other element in the sentence).

2.1. Coordinating Conjunctions

Different types of coordinating conjunctions are used to indicate, more precisely, the logical connection between elements in a sentence. Such logical connections include the following:

Copulative: καί ("and"), τε ("and"), οὐδέ ("and not/nor") used to link or to add a further element or idea.

> ὁ θεὸς τοῦ λαοῦ τούτου Ἰσραὴλ ἐξελέξατο τοὺς πατέρας ἡμῶν καὶ τὸν λαὸν ὕψωσεν ἐν τῇ παροικίᾳ ἐν γῇ Αἰγύπτου καὶ μετὰ βραχίονος ὑψηλοῦ ἐξήγαγεν αὐτοὺς ἐξ αὐτῆς "The God of this people Israel chose our fathers, and exalted the people in the land of Egypt, and with uplifted arm led them out of it" (Acts 13,17)

Adversative: ἀλλά ("but", for direct contrast), δέ ("but", for general contrast), πλήν ("but in any case"), μέν ... δέ ("on the one hand … on the other hand"), πλήν ("but, in any case"), ὅμως ("nevertheless"), καίτοι ("and yet") used to place two clauses in a contrastive relationship.

> ὁ μὲν θερισμὸς πολύς, οἱ δὲ ἐργάται ὀλίγοι "The harvest is great, but the laborers are few" (Matt 9,37)

Correlative: καί ... καί ("both … and"), οὔτε [μήτε] ... οὔτε [μήτε] ("neither … nor") used to place two clauses in a parallel relationship.

> ὅταν γὰρ ἐκ νεκρῶν ἀναστῶσιν οὔτε γαμοῦσιν οὔτε γαμίζονται "For when they rise from the dead, they neither marry nor are they given in marriage" (Mark 12,25)

Disjunctive: ἤ ("or"), ἤ ... ἤ ("either … or") used to identify two clauses as mutually exclusive alternatives.

> οὐδεὶς δύναται δυσὶ κυρίοις δουλεύειν· ἢ γὰρ τὸν ἕνα μισήσει καὶ τὸν ἕτερον ἀγαπήσει, ἢ ἑνὸς ἀνθέξεται καὶ τοῦ ἑτέρου καταφρονήσει "No one is able to serve two masters; for either he will hate the one and love the other, or he will be devoted to the one and despise the other" (Matt 6,24)

Inferential: ἄρα ("then"), διό, οὖν ("therefore") used to introduce the logical consequence of the preceding clause.

> εἰ δὲ Χριστὸς οὐκ ἐγήγερται, ματαία ἡ πίστις ὑμῶν, ἔτι ἐστὲ ἐν ταῖς ἁμαρτίαις ὑμῶν, ἄρα καὶ οἱ κοιμηθέντες ἐν Χριστῷ ἀπώλοντο "If Christ has not been raised, your faith is futile and you are still in your sins; then (consequently) those also who have fallen asleep in Christ have perished" (1 Cor 15,17-18)

Causal: γάρ ("for") used to introduce a statement that explains the cause or the basis of what was asserted earlier.

> καὶ ἐξεπλήσσοντο ἐπὶ τῇ διδαχῇ αὐτοῦ· ἦν γὰρ διδάσκων αὐτοὺς ὡς ἐξουσίαν ἔχων καὶ οὐχ ὡς οἱ γραμματεῖς "And they were

astonished at his teaching, for he was teaching them as one who had authority, and not as the scribes" (Mark 1,22)

2.2. Subordinating Conjunctions

Subordinating conjunctions can be divided according to the type of subordination that they establish between elements in the sentence:

Comparative: ὡς ("as"), ὥσπερ, καθώς ("just as") used to establish an analogy or a comparison between two elements in the sentence.

ἐπέπεσεν τὸ πνεῦμα τὸ ἅγιον ἐπ᾽ αὐτοὺς ὥσπερ καὶ ἐφ᾽ ἡμᾶς ἐν ἀρχῇ "The Holy Spirit fell upon them, just as [it fell] also upon us in the beginning" (Acts 11,15)

Conditional: εἰ, ἐάν ("if") used to introduce a condition that must be fulfilled before the action/state expressed in the conclusion can occur. For a more extensive discussion of Conditional Sentences, see Chapter Eight.

Temporal: ὅτε, ὁπότε ("when, while", simultaneous action), ἐπεί, ἐπειδή ("after", prior action), ἕως, μέχρι ("until", subsequent action) used to introduce a clause that stands in a temporal relationship with the main action of the sentence.

ἡμᾶς δεῖ ἐργάζεσθαι τὰ ἔργα τοῦ πέμψαντός με ἕως ἡμέρα ἐστίν· ἔρχεται νὺξ ὅτε οὐδεὶς δύναται ἐργάζεσθαι "It is necessary that we work the works of the one who sent me, while it is day; night comes, when no one can work" (John 9,4)

ἐπειδὴ ἐπλήρωσεν πάντα τὰ ῥήματα αὐτοῦ εἰς τὰς ἀκοὰς τοῦ λαοῦ, εἰσῆλθεν εἰς Καφαρναούμ "After he had completed all his words in the hearing of the people, he entered Capernaum" (Luke 7,1)

Final: ἵνα, ὅπως ("in order that") used to introduce a clause that states the intended goal or purpose of the agent of the main action of the sentence.

καὶ προσέφερον αὐτῷ παιδία ἵνα αὐτῶν ἅψηται "And they were bringing children to him, so that he might touch them" (Mark 10,13)

Consecutive: ὥστε, ὡς ("with the result that") to introduce a clause that expresses the outcome or the the result of the main action of the sentence.

καὶ συνέρχεται πάλιν ὁ ὄχλος, ὥστε μὴ δύνασθαι αὐτοὺς μηδὲ ἄρτον φαγεῖν "And again the crowd gathered, with the result that they were not able even to eat [bread]" (Mark 3,20)

οὕτως γὰρ ἠγάπησεν ὁ θεὸς τὸν κόσμον, ὥστε τὸν υἱὸν τὸν μονογενῆ ἔδωκεν "For God so loved the world, that he gave his only begotten son" (John 3,16)

Causal: ὅτι, διότι, ἐπεί, ἐπειδή ("because") used to introduce a clause that states the basis of an action or state.

δικαιωθέντες οὖν ἐκ πίστεως εἰρήνην ἔχομεν πρὸς τὸν θεὸν διὰ τοῦ κυρίου ἡμῶν Ἰησοῦ Χριστοῦ "Therefore, since we are justified by faith, we have peace with God through our Lord Jesus Christ" (Rom 5,1)

μὴ φοβοῦ, Ζαχαρία, διότι εἰσηκούσθη ἡ δέησίς σου "Do not fear, Zachariah, for your prayer has been heard" (Luke 1,13)

εἶπεν δὲ Μαριὰμ πρὸς τὸν ἄγγελον· πῶς ἔσται τοῦτο, ἐπεὶ ἄνδρα οὐ γινώσκω; "Mary said to the angel, 'How will this be, since I do not know a man?'" (Luke 1,34)

3. SENTENCE ADVERBS ("MODAL PARTICLES")

NT Greek is not rich in "modal particles" as compared with Classical Greek. Many of the Classical particles have dropped out of use, and those that remain have only a limited function.

3.1. Emphatic Particle: γε

In the NT, the particle γε ("at least") is used almost always in connection with other conjunctions. It serves to emphasize or intensify the meaning of the conjunction that precedes.

> εἰ ἄλλοις οὐκ εἰμὶ ἀπόστολος, ἀλλά γε ὑμῖν εἰμι "If to others I am not an apostle, *at least* I am to you" (1 Cor 9,2)

3.2. Interrogative Particles: οὐ, μή, μήτι, ἆρα

In rhetorical questions, the use of the particle οὐ indicates that the speaker expects an affirmative answer, whereas the use of μή or μήτι indicates that a negative answer is expected.

> μήτι δύναται τυφλὸς τυφλὸν ὁδηγεῖν; οὐχὶ ἀμφότεροι εἰς βόθυνον ἐμπεσοῦνται; "A blind man can't lead a blind man, can he?" [answer: "Certainly not!"] "Will they not both fall into a pit?" [answer: "Of course!"] (Luke 6,39)

The particle ἆρα is used to mark a neutral question. While not usually translated, it corresponds to the rise in inflection at the end of a spoken question.

> ὁ υἱὸς τοῦ ἀνθρώπου ἐλθὼν ἆρα εὑρήσει τὴν πίστιν ἐπὶ τῆς γῆς; "When the Son of Man comes, will he find faith on earth?" (Luke 18,8)

The particle εἰ is normally used to introduce an indirect question ("if, whether"), but in certain instances it simply marks the beginning of a direct question (cf. the analogous use of ὅτι [*recitativum*] to mark the beginning of a direct statement.

> καὶ ἐπηρώτησαν αὐτὸν λέγοντες· εἰ ἔξεστιν τοῖς σάββασιν θεραπεῦσαι; "And they asked him saying: 'Is it lawful to heal on the Sabbath?'" (Matt 12,10)

3.3. Asseverative Particles: ναί οὔ, οὐχί, δήπου

The particles, ναί ("yes") and οὔ / οὐχί ("no"), are used to introduce, respectively, a positive or negative asseveration.

> δοκεῖτε ὅτι εἰρήνην παρεγενόμην δοῦναι ἐν τῇ γῇ; οὐχί, λέγω ὑμῖν, ἀλλ' ἢ διαμερισμόν "Do you think that I have come to give peace on earth? No, I tell you, but rather division" (Luke 12,51)

> τί ἐξήλθατε ἰδεῖν; προφήτην; ναὶ λέγω ὑμῖν, καὶ περισσότερον προφήτου "What then did you go out to see? A prophet? Yes, I tell you, and more than a prophet" (Luke 7,26)

The particle, δήπου ("surely, of course"), is used in statements that appeal to widely held convictions. There is only one instance of this particle in the NT.

> οὐ γὰρ δήπου ἀγγέλων ἐπιλαμβάνεται ἀλλὰ σπέρματος Ἀβραὰμ ἐπιλαμβάνεται "For surely it is not with angels that he is concerned but with the descendants of Abraham" (Heb 2,16)

3.4. Modal Particle: ἄν

No separate word can be used to translate this particle by itself. Its force varies according to the mood of the verb it modifies. In general, ἄν limits the verb to particular conditions or circumstances: "in that case…".

4. SPECIAL USES OF COMMON PARTICLES

4.1. καί

In the NT the various conjunctional and adverbial uses of καί offer clear indications of Semitic influence (cf. syntactical uses of *waw*). Under this category may be listed the following uses:

4.1.1. Adversative καί ("and yet" or "but")

ἐμβλέψατε εἰς τὰ πετεινὰ τοῦ οὐρανοῦ, ὅτι οὐ σπείρουσιν, οὐδὲ θερίζουσιν, οὐδὲ συνάγουσιν εἰς ἀποθήκας, καὶ ὁ πατὴρ ὑμῶν ὁ οὐράνιος τρέφει αὐτά "Look at the birds of the sky, that they neither sow nor reap nor gather into barns, and yet your heavenly Father feeds them" (Matt 6,26)

ἐζήτουν αὐτὸν κρατῆσαι, καὶ ἐφοβήθησαν τὸν ὄχλον "They were trying to arrest him, but they feared the crowd" (Mark 12,12a)

4.1.2. Consecutive καί ("so that", "and so")

οὐδὲ καίουσιν λύχνον καὶ τιθέασιν αὐτὸν ὑπὸ τὸν μόδιον, ἀλλ' ἐπὶ τὴν λυχνίαν, καὶ λάμπει πᾶσιν τοῖς ἐν τῇ οἰκίᾳ "Nor do men light a lamp and put it under a bushel, but rather on a stand, so that it gives light to all in the house" (Matt 5,15)

4.1.3. Epexegetic καί ("that is")

οὕτως δὲ ἁμαρτάνοντες εἰς τοὺς ἀδελφοὺς καὶ τύπτοντες αὐτῶν τὴν συνείδησιν ἀσθενοῦσαν εἰς Χριστὸν ἁμαρτάνετε "Thus, sinning against your brothers, that is, wounding their conscience when it is weak, you sin against Christ" (1 Cor 8,12)

ὁ δὲ θεὸς δίδωσιν αὐτῷ σῶμα καθὼς ἠθέλησεν, καὶ ἑκάστῳ τῶν σπερμάτων ἴδιον σῶμα "But God gives it a body as he has chosen, that is, to each kind of seed its own body" (1 Cor 15,38)

4.1.4. Narrative καί (to introduce a main clause after a subordinate clause; cf. Hebrew "apodotic *waw*")

ὅτε ἐπλήσθησαν ἡμέραι ὀκτὼ τοῦ περιτεμεῖν αὐτόν, καὶ ἐκλήθη τὸ ὄνομα αὐτοῦ Ἰησοῦς "And when the eight days had passed for him to be circumcised, he was called Jesus by name" (Luke 2,21)

ὡς δὲ ἤγγισεν τῇ πύλῃ τῆς πόλεως, καὶ ἰδού, ἐξεκομίζετο τεθνηκώς, υἱὸς μονογενὴς τῇ μητρὶ αὐτοῦ "When he drew near to the gate of the city, behold, a man who had died was being carried out, the only son of his mother" (Luke 7,12)

ἐάν τις ἀκούσῃ τῆς φωνῆς μου καὶ ἀνοίξῃ τὴν θύραν, καὶ εἰσελεύσομαι πρὸς αὐτόν "If anyone hears my voice and opens the door, I will come in to him" (Rev 3,20)

4.2. δέ

The particle δέ is often used to connect one clause with another when there is some *general contrast* between them. It can also be used as a simple transitional particle to indicate the continuation of the discourse, or as an adverbial particle to introduce an explanation. Context will help to determine the intended sense.

4.2.1. Adversative sense of δέ ("but")

ὁ δὲ πνευματικὸς ἀνακρίνει μὲν πάντα, αὐτὸς δὲ ὑπ' οὐδενὸς ἀνακρίνεται "The spiritual man judges all things, but he himself is judged by no one" (1 Cor 2,15)

4.2.2. Progressive sense of δέ ("now then", "moreover")

οἴδαμεν δὲ ὅτι τοῖς ἀγαπῶσιν τὸν θεὸν πάντα συνεργεῖ εἰς ἀγαθόν "Now then we know that for those who love God all things work together for the good" (Rom 8,28)

4.2.3. Explanatory sense of δέ ("that is")

τί οὖν ἐροῦμεν; Ὅτι ἔθνη τὰ μὴ διώκοντα δικαιοσύνην, κατέλαβεν δικαιοσύνην, δικαιοσύνην δὲ τὴν ἐκ πίστεως; "What shall we say, then? That Gentiles who did not pursue righteousness have attained it, that is, righteousness through faith?" (Rom 9,30)

4.3. γάρ

The postpositive particle γάρ functions as a conjunction or as a sentence adverb ("modal particle") in the following ways:

1) to introduce a justifying cause of what was set forth in the preceding sentence (confirmatory sense)
2) to introduce an explanation of what was set forth in the preceding sentence (explanatory sense)
3) to express continuation or connection, often following an intervening interruption (progressive sense)

4.3.1. Confirmatory sense of γάρ ("for" or "since" or "as")

τέξεται δὲ υἱόν, καὶ καλέσεις τὸ ὄνομα αὐτοῦ Ἰησοῦν· αὐτὸς <u>γὰρ</u> σώσει τὸν λαὸν αὐτοῦ ἀπὸ τῶν ἁμαρτιῶν αὐτῶν "She will bear a son, and you shall call his name Jesus, <u>for</u> he will save his people from their sins" (Matt 1,21)

4.3.2. Explanatory sense of γάρ ("for, you see")

ἔρχεται γυνὴ ἐκ τῆς Σαμαρείας ἀντλῆσαι ὕδωρ. λέγει αὐτῇ ὁ Ἰησοῦς· δός μοι πεῖν· οἱ <u>γὰρ</u> μαθηταὶ αὐτοῦ ἀπεληλύθεισαν εἰς τὴν πόλιν ἵνα τροφὰς ἀγοράσωσιν "A Samaritan women came to draw water. Jesus said to her, 'Give me to drink'. <u>For</u> his disciples had gone away into the city to buy food" (John 4,7-8)

4.3.3. Progressive sense of γάρ ("and now" or "indeed" or "but")

Ἔτι <u>γὰρ</u> Χριστὸς ὄντων ἡμῶν ἀσθενῶν ἔτι κατὰ καιρὸν ὑπὲρ ἀσεβῶν ἀπέθανεν. μόλις <u>γὰρ</u> ὑπὲρ δικαίου τις ἀποθανεῖται· ὑπὲρ <u>γὰρ</u> τοῦ ἀγαθοῦ τάχα τις καὶ τολμᾷ ἀποθανεῖν· "<u>Now</u>, while we were still weak, at the right time Christ died for the ungodly. <u>Indeed</u>, one will hardly die for a righteous man, <u>but</u> perhaps for a good man one will dare to die" (Rom 5,6-7)

4.4. εἰ

As an interrogative particle, εἰ is used to introduce either a direct or an indirect question:

> εἶπεν δέ τις αὐτῷ, Κύριε, <u>εἰ</u> ὀλίγοι οἱ σῳζόμενοι; "Someone said to him, 'Lord, will those who are saved be few?" (Luke 13,23)

> Πιλάτος δὲ ἀκούσας Γαλιλαίαν ἐπηρώτησεν <u>εἰ</u> ὁ ἄνθρωπος Γαλιλαῖός ἐστιν "When Pilate heard mention of Galilee, he asked <u>whether</u> the man was a Galilean" (Luke 23,6)

It is also used to express *emphatic negation* in the (Hebraic) form of an oath with the imprecatory formula omitted: "[Let God strike me dead], *if* this happens" = "This *will not* happen".

> Τί ἡ γενεὰ αὕτη σημεῖον ἐπιζητεῖ; Ἀμὴν λέγω ὑμῖν, <u>εἰ</u> δοθήσεται τῇ γενεᾷ ταύτῃ σημεῖον "Why does this generation seek a sign? Truly, I say to you, [let God strike me dead] <u>if</u> a sign will be given to this generation [= no sign shall be given to this generation] (Mark 8,12)

4.5. ἵνα

Aside from its main use as a subordinating conjunction to introduce a purpose clause ("in order that..."), ἵνα also functions in the following ways:

1) to introduce a *noun clause* that serves as the subject or object of the main verb;
2) to introduce an *independent wish* or *exhortation*;
3) to introduce a *cause* or *reason* (equivalent to ὅτι).

4.5.1. ἵνα + noun clause

ἀλλ' ἐγὼ τὴν ἀλήθειαν λέγω ὑμῖν· συμφέρει ὑμῖν <u>ἵνα ἐγὼ ἀπέλθω</u> "But I tell you the truth: <u>that I go away</u> is beneficial to you" (John 16,7)

4.5.2. ἵνα independent wish or exhortation

ἕκαστος τὴν ἑαυτοῦ γυναῖκα οὕτως ἀγαπάτω ὡς ἑαυτόν· ἡ δὲ γυνὴ ἵνα φοβῆται τὸν ἄνδρα "Let each one of you love his own wife as himself; and the wife, let her respect her husband" (Eph 5,33)

ἐντολὴν καινὴν δίδωμι ὑμῖν, ἵνα ἀγαπᾶτε ἀλλήλους "I give you a new commandment: love one another" (John 13,34)

4.5.3. ἵνα + cause or reason

ἐν παραβολαῖς τὰ πάντα γίνεται· ἵνα βλέποντες βλέπωσιν, καὶ μὴ ἴδωσιν· καὶ ἀκούοντες ἀκούωσιν, καὶ μὴ συνιῶσιν
"All things are in parables, because in seeing they may see but not perceive, and in hearing they may hear but not understand" (Mark 4,11-12)

ἐν παραβολαῖς αὐτοῖς λαλῶ, ὅτι βλέποντες οὐ βλέπουσιν, καὶ ἀκούοντες οὐκ ἀκούουσιν, οὐδὲ συνιοῦσιν)
"I speak to them in parables, because seeing they do not see, and hearing they do not hear, nor understand" (Matt 13,13)

4.6. ὅτι

The subordinating conjunction, ὅτι is used to indicate either a *declarative* or a *causal* relationship between two clauses.

When used in a *declarative* sense ("that"), ὅτι introduces a *noun clause* that serves as the subject or object of the main verb.

οἱ δὲ ἐλθόντες λέγουσιν αὐτῷ, Διδάσκαλε, οἴδαμεν ὅτι ἀληθὴς εἶ "Those who came said to him, 'Teacher, we know that you are true'" (Mark 12,14) ὅτι δὲ ἐν νόμῳ οὐδεὶς δικαιοῦται παρὰ τῷ θεῷ, δῆλον "That no one is justified before God by the law is clear" (Gal 3,11)

When used in a *causal* sense ("because, since"), ὅτι introduces an *adverbial clause* that explains why something happened, or why a question is asked, or why something is known to be so.

καὶ διὰ τοῦτο ἐδίωκον τὸν Ἰησοῦν οἱ Ἰουδαῖοι, καὶ ἐζήτουν αὐτὸν ἀποκτεῖναι, ὅτι ταῦτα ἐποίει ἐν σαββάτῳ "For this reason the Jews were persecuting Jesus and trying to kill him, because he was doing these things on the Sabbath" (John 5,16)

οἱ δὲ ἄνθρωποι ἐθαύμασαν, λέγοντες, Ποταπός ἐστιν οὗτος, ὅτι καὶ οἱ ἄνεμοι καὶ ἡ θάλασσα ὑπακούουσιν αὐτῷ; "The men were astounded, saying, 'What sort of man is this, that both the winds and the sea obey him?'" (Matt 8,27)

εἶπον οὖν οἱ Ἰουδαῖοι πρὸς ἑαυτούς, Ποῦ οὗτος μέλλει πορεύεσθαι ὅτι ἡμεῖς οὐχ εὑρήσομεν αὐτόν; "Then the Jews were saying to one another, 'Where is he about to go, that we shall not find him?'" (John 7,35)

λέγω σοι, ἀφέωνται αἱ ἁμαρτίαι αὐτῆς αἱ πολλαί, ὅτι ἠγάπησεν πολύ· ᾧ δὲ ὀλίγον ἀφίεται, ὀλίγον ἀγαπᾷ "I say to you, her many sins are forgiven, because she loved much; but he to whom little is forgiven loves little" (Luke 7,47)

CHAPTER SEVEN
PREPOSITIONS

Select bibliography for further study: ABEL, *Grammaire*, 204-241; BEAL, G. K. – BRENDSEL, D. – ROSS, W., *An Interpretive Lexicon of the New Testament Greek. Analysis of Prepositions, Adverbs, Particles, Relative Pronouns, and Conjunctions* (Grand Rapids, MI 2014); BDF §§ 203-240; HARRIS, M. J., *Prepositions and Theology in the Greek New Testament: An Essential Reference Resource for Exegesis* (Grand Rapids, MI 2012); HOFFMANN – SIEBENTHAL, *Grammatik*, §§ 183-187; HUMBERT, *Syntaxe*, 298-344; MOULE, *Idiom-Book*, 48-92; MOULTON, *Prolegomena*, 98-107; MOULTON – TURNER, *Syntax*, 249-280; PORTER, *Idioms*, 139-180; ROBERTSON, *Grammar*, 553-649; SCHWYZER, *Grammatik*, 417-552; SMYTH, *Grammar*, §§ 1636-1702; WALLACE, *Grammar*, 355-389; YOUNG, *Intermediate*, 85-104; ZERWICK, *Biblical Greek*, §§ 78-135.

1. GENERAL INTRODUCTION

Prepositions are indeclinable words that are used in combination with a noun (in the genitive, dative, or accusative) to form a *prepositional phrase*. In some cases, the prepositional phrase gives further information about a noun in the sentence (*adjectival function*). More commonly, however, prepositional phrases have an *adverbial function*, i.e., they modify or determine in some way the action signified by the verb, answering the question: where? when? how? in what way/manner? with whom? etc. In general, prepositional phrases serve to express more precisely and effectively what simple case usage would communicate.

Prepositions that express *location/position* commonly take the dative case, whereas prepositions that express *motion toward* take the accusative, and those that express *motion away from* take the genitive. The chart below indicates the spatial function of the most common prepositions:

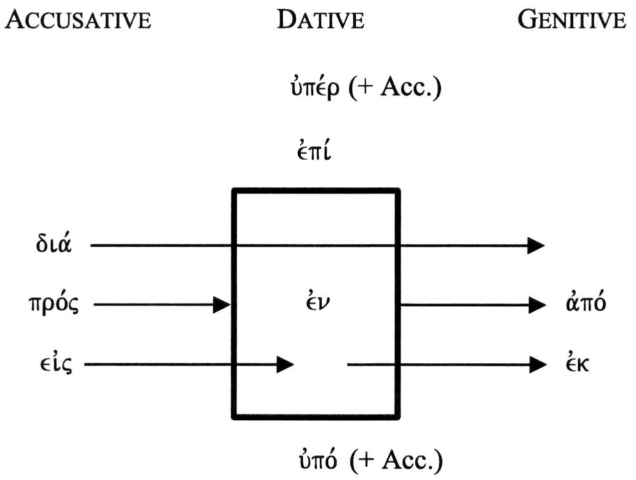

In general, prepositions expressing location/position are used with stative verbs, and prepositions expressing motion toward or motion away from are used to specify the direction of the movement expressed by verbs of motion, as in the following examples:

πᾶς ὁ ἐρχόμενος πρός με

ἐν τῇ συναγωγῇ ἦν ἄνθρωπος

ἀπελθεῖν ἀπὸ τῆς πόλεως

In certain instances, however, prepositions expressing location/position are used with verbs of motion, and, likewise, prepositions expressing motion/direction are used with stative verbs. In these cases, it is the semantic value of the verb that predominates, and the meaning of the prepositional phrase must be adjusted accordingly. Consider the following examples:

Ἐν ἀρχῇ ἦν ὁ λόγος, καὶ ὁ λόγος ἦν πρὸς τὸν θεόν, καὶ θεὸς ἦν ὁ λόγος "In the beginning was the Word, and the Word was with God, and the Word was God" (John 1,1)

καὶ ἤγετο ἐν τῷ πνεύματι ἐν τῇ ἐρήμῳ "And he was led by the Spirit in the desert" (Luke 4,1)

ἦν δὲ ὁ Φίλιππος ἀπὸ Βηθσαϊδά "And Philip was from Bethsaida" (John 1,44).

In comparison with Classical usage, the use of prepositions in the NT exhibits certain tendencies which can be observed in the LXX and also, in certain cases, in the secular writings of the Hellenistic period. These tendencies include the following:

- Reduced number of prepositions commonly used (from 17 to 7)
- Increased use of prepositions for the sake of greater clarity and vividness: e.g., λέγειν πρός τινα in place of λέγειν τινι
- Simplification in the use of prepositions with different cases: e.g., only ἐπί, παρά, and πρός are still used with genitive, dative, and accusative
- Loose interchange of prepositions with similar meanings: e.g., ἀπό (in place of ἐκ and ὑπό); ὑπέρ (in place of ἀντί and περί); εἰς (in place of πρός and ἐν)
- Increased use of certain adverbs as "improper prepositions" (always taking the genitive case):

ἄχρι "until; as far as"
ἔμπροσθεν "before"
ἕνεκεν (ἕνεκα) "on account of; because of; for the sake of"
ἐπάνω "over; above; on"
ἕως "until; up to"
μεταξύ "between; in the middle of"

ὄπισθεν "behind"
παρεκτός "apart from; except for"
πλήν "except"
ὑποκάτω "under; below"
χωρίς "apart from; without" (postpositive)

- Use of certain substantives referring to parts of the body (e.g., πρόσωπον, χείρ, στόμα) within prepositional phrases in imitation of Semitic formulations: e.g., ἀπὸ προσώπου (cf. מִפָּנִים); ἐν χειρί (cf. בְּיַד); διὰ στόματος

2. PREPOSITIONS WITH ONE CASE ONLY

2.1. With the Genitive

ἄνευ "without [the knowledge or consent of]"

ἀντί "in place of", "instead of"

ἀπό "from" in the sense required by the context: locative ("away from the exterior", but often used in place of ἐκ); partitive; separation; origin; cause; or agency (cf. ὑπό)

> κατ᾽ ἐκεῖνον δὲ τὸν καιρὸν ἐπέβαλεν Ἡρῴδης ὁ βασιλεὺς τὰς χεῖρας κακῶσαί τινας τῶν <u>ἀπὸ τῆς ἐκκλησίας</u> "At that time Herod the king laid hands on some of those <u>from the church</u>" (Acts 12,1)

> καὶ ἀναστὰς <u>ἀπὸ τῆς προσευχῆς</u>, ἐλθὼν πρὸς τοὺς μαθητὰς εὗρεν αὐτοὺς κοιμωμένους <u>ἀπὸ τῆς λύπης</u> "And getting up <u>from prayer</u> and coming to his disciples, he found them asleep <u>out of grief</u>" (Luke 22,45)

καὶ οἱ ἐνοχλούμενοι ἀπὸ πνευμάτων ἀκαθάρτων, καὶ ἐθεραπεύοντο "And those who were troubled with unclean spirits" (Luke 6,18)

ἄτερ "apart from", "without"

ἐκ "from" in the sense required by the context: separation ("out from the interior"); origin; source; cause; partitive; content (cf. genitive of fulness)

> καὶ ἰδού, φωνὴ ἐκ τῶν οὐρανῶν, λέγουσα, Οὗτός ἐστιν ὁ υἱός μου ὁ ἀγαπητός, ἐν ᾧ εὐδόκησα "And behold, there was a voice from heaven, saying, 'This is my beloved son, in whom I am well pleased'" (Matt 3,17).

> καὶ εἶπεν αὐτῷ Ναθαναήλ, ἐκ Ναζαρὲτ δύναταί τι ἀγαθὸν εἶναι; "And Nathanael said to him, 'Can something good come from Nazareth?'" (John 1,46)

> καὶ ἐπεθύμει γεμίσαι τὴν κοιλίαν αὐτοῦ ἐκ τῶν κερατίων "And he longed to fill his stomach with the pods" (Luke 15,16)

πρό "before" in a temporal or spatial sense; often replaced with adverbs used as improper propositions (+ genitive): e.g., ἔμπροσθεν, ἐνάντιον, ἐνώπιον, ἔναντι

> ὅτι ἠγάπησάς με πρὸ καταβολῆς κόσμου "Because you loved me before the foundation of the world" (John 17,24)

> ἦν ὁ Πέτρος κοιμώμενος μεταξὺ δύο στρατιωτῶν, δεδεμένος ἁλύσεσιν δυσίν· φύλακές τε πρὸ τῆς θύρας ἐτήρουν τὴν φυλακήν "And Peter was sleeping between two soldiers, bound with two chains, and the guards before the door were guarding the prison" (Acts 12,6)

2.2. With the Dative

ἐν "in" usually in a locative sense, but sometimes used in phrases that convey other uses of the dative: instrument or personal agency (cf. Hebrew uses of בְּ); accompaniment; respect; manner; time at which

> οἱ Φαρισαῖοι ἔλεγον, ἐν τῷ ἄρχοντι τῶν δαιμονίων ἐκβάλλει τὰ δαιμόνια "The Pharisees were saying, 'By the ruler of demons he casts out demons'" (Matt 9,34)
>
> λέγω ὑμῖν ὅτι ποιήσει τὴν ἐκδίκησιν αὐτῶν ἐν τάχει "I tell you that he will bring about their vindication quickly [= in haste]" (Luke 18,8)
>
> ἰδόντες δὲ οἱ περὶ αὐτὸν τὸ ἐσόμενον εἶπαν· κύριε, εἰ πατάξομεν ἐν μαχαίρῃ; "Those about him, seeing what was going to happen, said, 'Lord, shall we strike with the sword?'" (Luke 22,49)

σύν "with", often to express accompaniment, which in Classical Greek would be expressed with μετά + dative

2.3. With the Accusative

εἰς "into" in a directional sense, but also used in a variety of constructions to express: temporal limits ("up to" or "at") or duration ("during"); means or instrument; purpose or result; predicate nominative or accusative (cf. Hebrew uses of לְ)

> οἵτινες πληρωθήσονται εἰς τὸν καιρὸν αὐτῶν "[My words] which will be fulfilled in their [proper] time" (Luke 1,20)

ἐλάβετε τὸν νόμον εἰς διαταγὰς ἀγγέλων, καὶ οὐκ ἐφυλάξατε "You received the law through the direction of angels, but you did not keep it" (Acts 7,53)

ὁ υἱὸς τοῦ ἀνθρώπου παραδίδοται εἰς τὸ σταυρωθῆναι "The Son of man will be handed over to be crucified" (Matt 26,2)

Λίθον ὃν ἀπεδοκίμασαν οἱ οἰκοδομοῦντες, οὗτος ἐγενήθη εἰς κεφαλὴν γωνίας "The stone which the builders rejected, this stone has become the cornerstone" (Matt 21,42)

3. Prepositions with Two Cases

3.1. διά

With the Genitive: "through" in the sense required by the context: locative; temporal; instrument/personal agency

διὰ τῶν κεράμων καθῆκαν αὐτὸν σὺν τῷ κλινιδίῳ εἰς τὸ μέσον ἔμπροσθεν τοῦ Ἰησοῦ "They let him down with his bed through the tiles before Jesus" (Luke 5,19)

Ἐπιστάτα, δι᾽ ὅλης τῆς νυκτὸς κοπιάσαντες οὐδὲν ἐλάβομεν "Master, we toiled through the whole night and caught nothing" (Luke 5,5)

οὐδεὶς ἔρχεται πρὸς τὸν πατέρα, εἰ μὴ δι᾽ ἐμοῦ "No one comes to the Father except through me" (John 14,6)

With the Accusative: "on account of", "for the sake of", "because of"

Ἰησοῦς εἶπεν, Οὐ δι᾽ ἐμὲ αὕτη ἡ φωνὴ γέγονεν, ἀλλὰ δι᾽ ὑμᾶς "Jesus said, 'The voice has come not for my sake, but for your sake'" (John 12,30)

καὶ ἔσεσθε μισούμενοι ὑπὸ πάντων διὰ τὸ ὄνομά μου "And you will be hated by all because of my name" (Matt 10,22)

3.2. κατά

With the Genitive: "down from", "against", "by" (in oaths)

καὶ ὥρμησεν ἡ ἀγέλη κατὰ τοῦ κρημνοῦ εἰς τὴν θάλασσαν "And the herd rushed down the steep bank into the sea" (Mark 5,13)

ὅταν στήκητε προσευχόμενοι, ἀφίετε εἴ τι ἔχετε κατά τινος "Whenever you stand praying, forgive if you have something against someone" (Mark 11,25)

With the Accusative: "according to", but also used in a variety of constructions to express: spatial or temporal extension ("through", "along", "over"); direction ("to", "toward", "up to"); distribution ("in every"), goal or purpose ("for"), relationship ("in relation to", "in accordance with")

καὶ ἀπῆλθεν, καθ᾽ ὅλην τὴν πόλιν κηρύσσων ὅσα ἐποίησεν αὐτῷ ὁ Ἰησοῦς "And he went away, proclaiming throughout the whole city all that Jesus had done for him" (Luke 8,39)

κατὰ δὲ τὸ μεσονύκτιον Παῦλος καὶ Σίλας προσευχόμενοι ὕμνουν τὸν θεόν "And about midnight Paul and Silas were praying and singing hymns to God" (Acts 16,25)

κατὰ δὲ ἑορτὴν ἀπέλυεν αὐτοῖς ἕνα δέσμιον "At each feast he used to release to them a prisoner" (Mark 15,6) κατὰ τὴν πίστιν ὑμῶν γενηθήτω "Let it be done according to your faith" (Matt 9,29)

3.3. μετά

With the Genitive: "with" in the sense of accompaniment or attendant circumstances

κατέβη μετ' αὐτῶν, καὶ ἦλθεν εἰς Ναζαρέτ "He went down with them, and he came to Nazareth" (Luke 2,51)

ἐξελθοῦσαι ταχὺ ἀπὸ τοῦ μνημείου μετὰ φόβου καὶ χαρᾶς μεγάλης "They quickly came out of the tomb with fear and great joy" (Matt 28,8)

With the Accusative: "after" in a temporal sense

ὑμεῖς δὲ βαπτισθήσεσθε ἐν πνεύματι ἁγίῳ οὐ μετὰ πολλὰς ταύτας ἡμέρας "You will be baptized with the Holy Spirit not after many days" (Acts 1,5)

3.4. περί

With the Genitive: "about", "concerning" (an object of thought or speech)

ἐπίστευσαν τῷ Φιλίππῳ εὐαγγελιζομένῳ τὰ περὶ τῆς βασιλείας τοῦ θεοῦ "They believed Philip as he preached the good news about the kingdom of God" (Acts 8,12)

ἐγὼ περὶ αὐτῶν ἐρωτῶ· οὐ περὶ τοῦ κόσμου ἐρωτῶ "I am praying for them; I am not praying for the world" (John 17,9)

With the Accusative: "around" (place), "about" (time), "concerning" (object of action/effort) ἰδὼν ὁ Ἰησοῦς πολλοὺς ὄχλους περὶ αὐτόν, ἐκέλευσεν ἀπελθεῖν εἰς τὸ πέραν "Seeing the great crowds all around him, Jesus ordered to go to the other side" (Matt 8,18)

ἡ δὲ Μάρθα περιεσπᾶτο περὶ πολλὴν διακονίαν "And Martha was preoccupied with much serving" (Luke 10,40)

3.5. ὑπέρ

With the Genitive: "on behalf of", "for the sake of"

προσεύχεσθε ὑπὲρ τῶν διωκόντων ὑμᾶς "Pray for those who persecute you" (Matt 5,44)

With the Accusative: "beyond", "over", "above"

οὐκέτι ὡς δοῦλον, ἀλλ' ὑπὲρ δοῦλον, ἀδελφὸν ἀγαπητόν "He is no longer as a slave, but more than a slave, a beloved brother" (Phlm 16)

3.6. ὑπό

With the Genitive: "by" (agent of passive verb, often replaced by ἀπό)

πάντα μοι παρεδόθη ὑπὸ τοῦ πατρός μου "All things have been given over to me by my Father" (Matt 11,27)

With the Accusative: "under" (spatial)

οὐδὲ καίουσιν λύχνον καὶ τιθέασιν αὐτὸν ὑπὸ τὸν μόδιον "Nor do they light a lamp and place it under a bushel" (Matt 5,15)

4. PREPOSITIONS WITH THREE CASES

4.1. ἐπί

With the Genitive: "on, upon" (spatial), "at" (temporal), "before" (with persons), "over" (of authority)

γενηθήτω τὸ θέλημά σου, ὡς ἐν οὐρανῷ, καὶ ἐπὶ τῆς γῆς "Let your will be done, as in heaven also on earth" (Matt 6,10)

καὶ εἰς συναγωγὰς δαρήσεσθε, καὶ ἐπὶ ἡγεμόνων καὶ βασιλέων σταθήσεσθε ἕνεκεν ἐμοῦ "You will be beaten in synagogues, and you be made to stand before governors and kings for my sake" (Mark 13,9)

ἀνὴρ Αἰθίοψ εὐνοῦχος δυνάστης Κανδάκης τῆς βασιλίσσης Αἰθιόπων, ὃς ἦν ἐπὶ πάσης τῆς γάζης αὐτῆς "An Ethiopian, a eunuch, a minister of Candace, queen of the Ethiopians, who had charge over all her treasure" (Acts 8,27)

With the Dative: "upon" (spatial), "over" (of authority), "on" (to indicate the basis or reason for a fact or action)

ὅταν ἴδητε ταῦτα πάντα, γινώσκετε ὅτι ἐγγύς ἐστιν ἐπὶ θύραις "When you see these things, know that he is near at the gates" (Matt 24,33)

ἐπὶ πᾶσιν τοῖς ὑπάρχουσιν αὐτοῦ καταστήσει αὐτόν "He will set him over all his possessions (Luke 12,44)

ἐπὶ δὲ τῷ ῥήματί σου χαλάσω τὸ δίκτυον "At your word [= on the authority of your word] I will lower the nets" (Luke 5,5)

With the Accusative: "on, towards" (spatial), "at" (temporal), "over" (of authority), "to, for" (to indicate intention or purpose)

οὐδὲ καίουσιν λύχνον καὶ τιθέασιν αὐτὸν ὑπὸ τὸν μόδιον, ἀλλ' ἐπὶ τὴν λυχνίαν "Nor do men light a lamp and place it under a bushel, but [instead] on a lampstand" (Matt 5,15)

ὁ δὲ Ἰησοῦς [...] εἶπεν, σπλαγχνίζομαι ἐπὶ τὸν ὄχλον "Jesus said, 'I have compassion on the crowd'" (Matt 15,32)

Πέτρος καὶ Ἰωάννης ἀνέβαινον εἰς τὸ ἱερὸν ἐπὶ τὴν ὥραν τῆς προσευχῆς "Peter and John went up to the temple at the hour of prayer" (Acts 3,1)

καὶ βασιλεύσει ἐπὶ τὸν οἶκον Ἰακὼβ εἰς τοὺς αἰῶνας "And he will rule over the house of Jacob for ever" (Luke 1,33)

4.2. παρά

With the Genitive: "from [the side of]"

πεπιστεύκατε ὅτι ἐγὼ παρὰ τοῦ θεοῦ ἐξῆλθον "You have believed that I came from the Father" (John 16,27)

With the Dative: "by", "before", "near", "beside"

εἱστήκεισαν δὲ παρὰ τῷ σταυρῷ τοῦ Ἰησοῦ ἡ μήτηρ αὐτοῦ, καὶ ἡ ἀδελφὴ τῆς μητρὸς αὐτοῦ "Standing beside the cross of Jesus were his mother and his mother's sister" (John 19,25)

οὐ γὰρ οἱ ἀκροαταὶ τοῦ νόμου δίκαιοι παρὰ τῷ θεῷ "For the hearers of the Law are not righteous before God" (Rom 2,13).

With the Accusative: "along the side of", "against", "other than"

καὶ ἐν τῷ σπείρειν αὐτόν, ἃ μὲν ἔπεσεν παρὰ τὴν ὁδόν "And while he sowed, some [of the seed] fell along the side of the road" (Matt 13,4) αἳ θήλειαι αὐτῶν μετήλλαξαν τὴν φυσικὴν χρῆσιν εἰς τὴν παρὰ φύσιν "Their women exchanged natural relations for those contrary to nature" (Rom 1,26)

ἐὰν ἡμεῖς ἢ ἄγγελος ἐξ οὐρανοῦ εὐαγγελίζηται ὑμῖν παρ' ὃ εὐηγγελισάμεθα ὑμῖν, ἀνάθεμα ἔστω "If we or an angel from heaven preaches to you a gospel contrary to the one which we preached to you, let him be accursed" (Gal 1,8)

4.3. πρός

With the Genitive: "on the side of", "in the interest of", "to the advantage of"

διὸ παρακαλῶ ὑμᾶς προσλαβεῖν τροφῆς· τοῦτο γὰρ πρὸς τῆς ὑμετέρας σωτηρίας ὑπάρχει "Therefore I urge you to take food, for this is for your salvation" (Acts 27,34)

With the Dative: "near", "at", "by"

ἦν δὲ ἐκεῖ πρὸς τῷ ὄρει ἀγέλη χοίρων μεγάλη "There on the hillside was a great herd of swine" (Mark 5,11)

With the Accusative: "to" (with verbs of motion, sending, speaking), "near, at, by" (locatve); "for" (to express purpose or result), "with regard to", "in accordance with"

δεῦτε πρός με πάντες οἱ κοπιῶντες καὶ πεφορτισμένοι, κἀγὼ ἀναπαύσω ὑμᾶς "Come to me all you who labor and are burdened, and I will give you rest" (Matt 11,28)

ἐν ἀρχῇ ἦν ὁ λόγος, καὶ ὁ λόγος ἦν πρὸς τὸν θεόν, καὶ θεὸς ἦν ὁ λόγος "In the beginning was the Word, and the Word was with God, and the Word was God" (John 1,1)

προσέχετε τὴν ἐλεημοσύνην ὑμῶν μὴ ποιεῖν ἔμπροσθεν τῶν ἀνθρώπων, πρὸς τὸ θεαθῆναι "Beware not to practice your piety before men, so as to be seen by them" (Matt 6,1) ἑκάστῳ δὲ δίδοται ἡ φανέρωσις τοῦ πνεύματος πρὸς τὸ συμφέρον "To each is given the manifestation of the Spirit for the common good (1 Cor 12,7)

CHAPTER EIGHT
CONDITIONAL SENTENCES

Select bibliography for further study: ABEL, *Grammaire*, 287-290; ARMITAGE, D.J., "An Exploration of Conditional Clause Exegesis with Reference to Galatians 1,8-9", *Bib* 88 (2007) 365-392; BDF §§ 360, 371-376, 454, 417; BOYER, J.L., "First Class Conditions. What do they mean?", *GTJ* 2 (1981) 75-114; IDEM, "Second Class Conditions in New Testament Greek", *GTJ* 3 (1982) 81-88; IDEM, "Third (and Fourth) Class Conditions", *GTJ* 3 (1982) 163-175; IDEM, "Other Conditional Elements in New Testament Greek", *GTJ* 4 (1983) 173-188; HOFFMANN – SIEBENTHAL, *Grammatik*, §§ 280-285; HUMBERT, *Syntaxe*, 219-225; MOULE, *Idiom-Book*, 148-152; MOULTON – TURNER, *Syntax*, 113-116; PORTER, *Idioms*, 254-267; ROBERTSON, *Grammar*, 1004-1027; SCHWYZER, *Grammatik*, 682-688; SMYTH, *Grammar*, §§ 2280-2368; WALLACE, *Grammar*, 679-712; YOUNG, *Intermediate*, 225-230; ZERWICK, *Biblical Greek*, §§ 299-334.

1. GENERAL INTRODUCTION

A *conditional sentence* is a complex sentence consisting of two clauses: the *protasis* and the *apodosis*. The protasis derives its name from πρότασις, meaning "stretching forward" or "that which is put forward" (in logic, a *premise*). In a conditional sentence, the protasis is the conditional (subordinate) clause that expresses a supposed or assumed case ("if A . . ."). The apodosis, on the other hand, takes its name from ἀπόδοσις, which means "giving back, return". In a conditional sentence, the apodosis is the principal clause stating the conclusion that follows when the condition is fulfilled or realized ("then B . . ."). The protasis can be stated either before or after the apodosis, with no difference in meaning:

> If it rains today (*protasis*), they will not go to school (*apodosis*).
> They will not go to school (*apodosis*), if it rains today (*protasis*).

The negative of the protasis is μή, since the subordinate clause expresses a possibility that is conceived or imagined. The negative of the apodosis is οὐ, since the principal clause states the conclusion as a *fact* on the supposition that the protasis is true.

Conditional sentences can be classified according to the type of condition that is expressed [5] :

1) a probable or possible occurrence in the future;
2) a simple or general occurrence in the present;
3) an unreal occurrence contrary to what is known to be true in the present or in the past.

Six different types of conditional sentences are most commonly used, each with its own way of formulating the protasis and apodosis.

1.1. Future More Vivid Conditional Sentence
1.2. Future Less Vivid Conditional Sentence
2.1. Present Simple Conditional Sentence
2.2. Present General Conditional Sentence
3.1. Present Contrafactual Conditional Sentence
3.2. Past Contrafactual Conditional Sentence

A translation formula (with the verb "do") is provided below for each type of conditional sentence. These formulas will help to clarify how the expressed condition is to be understood. It must be noted that sometimes

---

[5] There is a long-standing debate over how best to classify conditional sentences in ancient Greek. Some scholars maintain that proper categories emerge from a close analysis of formal features alone, such as the use of ἐάν vs. εἰ and the choice of moods and tenses. Others begin with an analysis of formal features but then give greater consideration to general semantic issues, such as the type of condition expressed (e.g., particular or general, present or future) and the logical connection between the protasis and apodosis.

the protasis of one type of conditional sentence is combined with the apodosis of another type. This results in a *mixed conditional sentence.* In such cases, the translation formula for the protasis of one type of conditional sentence is to be combined with the translation formula for the apodosis of the other type.

2. FUTURE CONDITIONS

Future conditions set forth suppositions that may or may not be realized. There are two main forms of future conditions: *Future More Vivid* and *Future Less Vivid.* The difference depends on how the speaker views the condition. In a *Future More Vivid* conditional sentence, the speaker expresses in the protasis what he views *vividly* and *distinctly* in his mind as something that is likely to occur. In a *Future Less Vivid* conditional sentence, on the other hand, the speaker states in the protasis what he views only *vaguely* and *indistinctly* as something that may possibly occur.

2.1. Future More Vivid Conditional Sentence

Protasis: ἐάν ("if") + Subjunctive (Present or Aorist)
Apodosis: Future Indicative (or equivalent)
Translation formula: *does / will do*

> ἐὰν ὁ θεὸς ἄγγελον πέμπῃ (πέμψῃ), τοὺς λόγους αὐτοῦ πιστεύσουσιν
> "If God sends an angel, they will believe his words"

The protasis of the Future More Vivid Conditional Sentence makes an assumption about what the speaker thinks is likely to happen in the future, and the apodosis draws a conclusion based on the realization of that assumption. In the protasis, the choice between the present or aorist subjunctive depends on the aspect of the action as envisioned by the speaker. While the verb in the apodosis is normally the future indicative, it may also be expressed in any form of the simple sentence that refers to the future (e.g., a command expressed in the Imperative). In addition to the regular formulation with ἐάν (= εἰ + ἄν), the protasis can be introduced also by a form of the relative pronoun + ἄν.

> ὃν ἂν ὁ θεὸς πέμπῃ, ἐκεῖνος πιστευθήσεται
> "Whomever God sends [If God sends anyone], that one will be believed"

2.2. Future Less Vivid Conditional Sentence

Protasis: εἰ ("if") + Optative (Present or Aorist)
Apodosis: Optative (Present or Aorist) + ἄν
Translation formula: *should do / would do*

> εἰ ὁ θεὸς ἄγγελον πέμποι (πέμψαι), τοὺς λόγους αὐτοῦ πιστεύοιεν (πιστεύσαιεν) ἄν
> "If God should send an angel, they would believe his words"

The protasis of a Future Less Vivid Conditional Sentence makes an assumption about what may or may not occur in the future, and the apodosis draws a conclusion based on this indefinite assumption. In both the protasis and the apodosis, the choice between the present and aorist optative depends upon the aspect of the action as envisioned by the speaker. The modal particle ἄν is an essential part of the formulation of the apodosis, but it is not separately translated. In addition to the regular formulation (with εἰ), the protasis can be introduced also by a form of the relative pronoun.

> ὃν ὁ θεὸς πέμποι (πέμψαι), ἐκεῖνος πιστεύοιτο (πιστευθείη) ἄν
> "Whomever God should send [If God should send anyone], that one would be believed"

3. PRESENT CONDITIONS: SIMPLE AND GENERAL

A simple condition refers to a definite action or to several definite actions occurring at a definite time. A general condition refers to any one of a series of actions that may occur at any time.

3.1. Present Simple Conditional Sentence

Protasis: εἰ ("if") + Present Indicative
Apodosis: Present Indicative (or equivalent)
Translation formula: *does / does*

> εἰ ὁ θεὸς ἄγγελον πέμπει, πιστεύουσιν τοὺς λόγους αὐτοῦ
> "If God sends an angel, they believe his words"

The protasis of a Simple Conditional Sentence states a simple assumption with emphasis on the reality of the assumption (*not* on the reality of what is being assumed). The condition is considered "a real case". The apodosis commonly has the indicative, but also any other form of the simple sentence appropriate to the thought. The protasis can be introduced also by a form of the relative pronoun.

> ὃν ὁ θεὸς πέμπει, πιστεύουσιν τοὺς λόγους αὐτοῦ
> "Whomever God sends [If God sends anyone], they believe his words"

3.2. Present General Conditional Sentence

Protasis: ἐάν ("if") + Subjunctive (Present or Aorist)
Apodosis: Present Indicative
Translation formula: *(ever) does / (always) does*

> ἐὰν ὁ θεὸς ἄγγελον πέμπῃ (πέμψῃ), τοὺς λόγους αὐτοῦ πιστεύουσιν
> "If [ever] God sends an angel, they [always] believe his words"

The protasis of a General Conditional Sentence makes an assumption about what may occur in the present. The protasis has the force of "*if ever*" or "*whenever*", while the apodosis states the conclusion that ("*always*") follows *as a general rule*. The choice between the present or aorist subjunctive in the protasis depends on the aspect of the action as envisioned by the speaker. While the form of the protasis is the same as that for a Future More Vivid Conditional Sentence (ἐάν + Subjunctive), the use of the Present Indicative in the apodosis indicates the difference. The protasis can be introduced by a form of the relative pronoun + ἄν.

> ὃν ἂν ὁ θεὸς πέμπῃ, ἐκεῖνος πιστεύεται
> "Whomever God sends [If ever God sends anyone], that one is [always] believed"

4. CONTRAFACTUAL (UNREAL) CONDITIONS

In contrafactual conditional sentences, the protasis sets forth a supposition that is contrary to a known fact. In the apodosis, the speaker states what *would be* or what *would have been* the result if the condition were, or had been, realized.

4.1. Present Contrafactual Conditional Sentence

Protasis: εἰ ("if") + Imperfect Indicative
Apodosis: Imperfect Indicative + ἄν
Translation formula: *were doing / would be doing*

> εἰ ὁ θεὸς ἄγγελον ἔπεμπεν, τοὺς λόγους αὐτοῦ ἐπίστευον ἄν
> "If God were sending an angel [but He is not], they would be believing his words"

The protasis of a Present Contrafactual Conditional Sentence makes an assumption about something that the speaker knows is untrue at the present time, and the apodosis draws a conclusion based on this unreal assumption. In this type of conditional sentence, the indicative mood is used to describe an *unreal* action or state of being. The protasis can be introduced also by a form of the relative pronoun.

> ὃν ὁ θεὸς ἔπεμπεν, ἐκεῖνος ἐπιστεύετο ἄν
> "If God were sending anyone (but He is not), that one would be believed"

4.2. Past Contrafactual Conditional Sentence

Protasis: εἰ ("if") + Aorist Indicative
Apodosis: Aorist Indicative + ἄν
Translation formula: *had done / would have done*

> εἰ ὁ θεὸς ἄγγελον ἔπεμψεν, τοὺς λόγους αὐτοῦ ἐπίστευσαν ἄν
> "If God had sent an angel [but He did not], they would have believed his words"

The protasis of a Past Contrafactual Conditional Sentence makes an assumption about something the speaker knows was untrue in the past, and the apodosis draws a conclusion based on this unreal assumption. The protasis can be introduced also by a form of the relative pronoun.

> ὃν ὁ θεὸς ἔπεμψεν, ἐκεῖνος ἐπιστεύθη ἄν
> "If God had sent anyone [but He did not], that one would have been believed"

SUMMARY OF CONDITIONAL SENTENCES

Future More Vivid Condition

Protasis: ἐάν + SUBJUNCTIVE *"does"* Apodosis: FUTURE INDICATIVE *"will do"*

ἐὰν ἀγαπᾶτέ με, τὰς ἐντολὰς τὰς ἐμὰς τηρήσατε
"If you love me, then observe my commandments" (John 14,15)

Future Less Vivid Condition

Protasis: εἰ + OPTATIVE *"should do"* Apodosis: OPTATIVE + ἄν *"would do"*

No clear instance of this type of conditional sentence is found in the NT, with the possible exception of 1 Peter 3,14: εἰ καὶ πάσχοιτε διὰ δικαιοσύνην, μακάριοι ("If you should suffer on account of righteousness, then blessed [are you]").

Present Simple Condition

Protasis: εἰ + INDICATIVE *"does"* Apodosis: INDICATIVE *"does"*

εἰ δὲ πνεύματι ἄγεσθε, οὐκ ἐστὲ ὑπὸ νόμον
"If you are led by the Spirit, you are not under the law" (Gal 5,18)

Present General Condition

Protasis: ἐάν + SUBJUNCTIVE *"does"* Apodosis: PRESENT INDICATIVE *"does"*

ἐὰν μὴ ὁ κόκκος τοῦ σίτου πεσὼν εἰς τὴν γῆν ἀποθάνῃ, αὐτὸς μόνος μένει· ἐὰν δὲ ἀποθάνῃ, πολὺν καρπὸν φέρει
"If a grain of wheat does not fall into the earth and die, then it remains alone; but if it dies, then it bears much fruit" (John 12,24)

Present Contrafactual Condition

Protasis: εἰ + IMP. INDIC. — *"were doing"*

Apodosis: IMP. INDIC. + ἄν — *"would be doing"*

εἰ ἐκ τοῦ κόσμου τούτου ἦν ἡ βασιλεία ἡ ἐμή, οἱ ὑπηρέται ἂν οἱ ἐμοὶ ἠγωνίζοντο
"If my kingdom were of this world, then my servants would be fighting" (John 18,36)

Past Contrafactual Condition

Protasis: εἰ + AORIST INDIC. — *"had done"*

Apodosis: AORIST IND. + ἄν — *"would have done"*

εἰ ἐν Τύρῳ καὶ Σιδῶνι ἐγένοντο αἱ δυνάμεις αἱ γενόμεναι ἐν ὑμῖν, πάλαι ἂν ἐν σάκκῳ καὶ σποδῷ μετενόησαν
"If the mighty works done in your midst had been done in Tyre and Sidon, then they would have repented long ago in sackcloth and ashes" (Matt 11,21)

CHAPTER NINE
SEMITIC INFLUENCE ON NT GREEK

Select bibliography for further study: BLACK, M., *An Aramaic Approach to the Gospels and Acts* (Oxford [3]1967); BDF §§ 4 *et passim*; MOULE, *Idiom-Book*, 171-191; MOULTON, *Prolegomena*, 10-19; MOULTON – HOWARD, *Accidence and Word Formation*, 412-485; ROBERTSON, *Grammar*, 88-108; SILVA, M., "Bilingualism and the Character of New Testament Greek", *Bib* 69 (1980) 198-219; WILCOX, M., «Semitism in the New Testament», *ANRW* II.25.2 (1984) 978-1029; ZERWICK, *Biblical Greek*, §§ 480-494 *et passim*.

1. GENERAL INTRODUCTION

It is indisputable that the writings of the NT include a variety of words, phrases, and grammatical constructions that are unusual in Greek but very similar to corresponding expressions in Hebrew and Aramaic. These peculiarities are called "Semitisms", and they reflect the influence of Semitic languages on the Greek of Jewish and Christian authors of the time. Some of the Semitisms in the NT are to be viewed as "Septuagintisms", for they are found in explicit citations of texts from the LXX, or in passages where the NT author is deliberately imitating an expression or formulation commonly used in the LXX. In addition to these instances of "biblical Greek", some of the Semitisms in the NT reflect the influence of spoken Aramaic on the popular (vulgar) Greek of the NT authors, a phenomenon called "linguistic interference". In certain cases, a high concentration of Semitic words and expressions in a NT text may indicate the author's reliance on an underlying source that was originally written in Aramaic.

2. CASE USAGE

2.1. Pendent Nominative

The Pendent Nominative is a type of anacolouthon (i.e., a break in the grammar of a sentence). It occurs when a noun in the nominative case is left hanging in suspension (*pendens*), because it names as the main topic a person or thing other than the subject of the verb in the sentence that follows. This manner of expression, while ungrammatical, is very common in ordinary speech: e.g., "That guy standing in the piazza, I met him two years ago in Milan". While not without parallel in vulgar Greek, the Pendent Nominative is used frequently in the LXX to render the corresponding Semitic construction. Therefore, some uses of the Pendent Nominative in the NT may be viewed as Septuagintisms, while others seem to reflect the influence of this common Semitic construction on the colloquial style of the NT authors.

> ὁ γὰρ Μωϋσῆς οὗτος, ὃς ἐξήγαγεν ἡμᾶς ἐκ γῆς Αἰγύπτου, οὐκ οἴδαμεν τί ἐγένετο αὐτῷ "For this Moses, who led us out of the land of Egypt, we do not know what happened to him" (Acts 7,40; cf. LXX Exod 32,23)

> ὁ θέλων σοι κριθῆναι καὶ τὸν χιτῶνά σου λαβεῖν, ἄφες αὐτῷ καὶ τὸ ἱμάτιον "The one who wants to sue you and take your tunic, give to him also your cloak" (Matt 5,40 D)

2.2. Hebrew Genitive (Genitive of Quality or Adjectival Genitive)

The Hebrew Genitive consists in the use of the genitive to denote a quality or attribute of another noun (the *nomen regens*). This use of the genitive comes closest to that of the simple adjective. The frequency of this usage in the NT, especially in places where a Greek-speaker would normally use an adjective, may be attributed to the influence of Semitic languages, in which attributes or qualities are commonly expressed with a noun in the genitive case, and not with an adjective.

> ἐθαύμαζον ἐπὶ τοῖς λόγοις τῆς χάριτος "They were amazed at his gracious words [lit., words of grace]" (Luke 4,22)

> καὶ ἐγὼ ὑμῖν λέγω, ἑαυτοῖς ποιήσατε φίλους ἐκ τοῦ μαμωνᾶ τῆς ἀδικίας "And I say to you, make friends for yourselves out of unrighteous mammon [lit., mammon of unrighteousness]" (Luke 16,9)

> διὰ τοῦτο παρέδωκεν αὐτοὺς ὁ θεὸς εἰς πάθη ἀτιμίας "For this reason God gave them up to dishonorable passions [lit., passions of dishonor]" (Rom 1,26)

Analogous to the Hebrew Genitive is the use of forms of υἱός with the genitive of a person or thing. In this usage, which is prominently but not exclusively Semitic, the genitive denotes a close relationship that characterizes the one named as υἱός.

> τὸ δὲ καλὸν σπέρμα οὗτοί εἰσιν οἱ υἱοὶ τῆς βασιλείας· τὰ δὲ ζιζάνιά εἰσιν οἱ υἱοὶ τοῦ πονηροῦ "These are the good seed, the sons of the Kingdom, and the weeds are the sons of the evil one (Matt 13,38)

> οἱ υἱοὶ τοῦ αἰῶνος τούτου φρονιμώτεροι ὑπὲρ τοὺς υἱοὺς τοῦ φωτός "The sons of this age are more clever than the sons of light" (Luke 16,8)

> γινώσκετε ἄρα ὅτι οἱ ἐκ πίστεως, οὗτοι υἱοί εἰσιν Ἀβραάμ "So you see that it is the men of faith, these are the sons of Abraham" (Gal 3,7)

2.3. Cognate Dative

The dative of a verbal noun is sometimes used with the finite form of a cognate verb to express an intensified action. While not without parallel in Greek, this construction closely resembles the Hebrew use of the Infinitive Absolute to strengthen the idea of the verb, as in Gen 2,17 (MT): מוֹת תָּמוּת ("you shall surely die").

ἐπιθυμίᾳ ἐπεθύμησα τοῦτο τὸ πάσχα φαγεῖν μεθ' ὑμῶν πρὸ τοῦ με παθεῖν "I have greatly desired [lit., "with a desire I have desired"] to eat this Passover with you before I suffer" (Luke 22,15)

παραγγελίᾳ παρηγγείλαμεν ὑμῖν μὴ διδάσκειν ἐπὶ τῷ ὀνόματι τούτῳ "we strictly ordered [lit., "with an order we ordered"] you not to teach in this name" (Acts 5,28)

When an attribute is added to the cognate verbal noun, the accusative case is preferred.

ἰδόντες δὲ τὸν ἀστέρα ἐχάρησαν χαρὰν μεγάλην σφόδρα "Upon seeing the star, they rejoiced exceedingly with a great joy" (Matt 2,10)

3. USES OF THE DEFINITE ARTICLE

In general, the use of the definite article in the NT conforms to the rules of good Greek style. There are, however, several exceptional cases in which the definite article is omitted even though the speaker is referring to a specific person or thing. Such anarthrous formulations are in imitation of the Semitic construct chain, in which the *nomen regens* is defined, not by the use of the definite article (הָ), but, instead, by the *nomen rectum* that follows. The imitation of the Semitic construct chain is certainly evident in several fixed prepositional phrases in which the *nomen regens* (without the definite article) is defined by the genitive that follows.

διὰ σπλάγχνα ἐλέους θεοῦ ἡμῶν "through *the* organ of mercy of our God" (Luke 1,78)

ἐκ κοιλίας μητρὸς αὐτοῦ "from *the* womb of his mother" (Matt 19,12)

ἐν βίβλῳ λόγων Ἠσαΐου τοῦ προφήτου "in *the* book of the words of Isaiah the prophet" (Luke 3,4) εἰς οἶκόν τινος τῶν ἀρχόντων "into *the* house of one of the leaders" (Luke 14,1)

ἐν ἡμέρᾳ ὀργῆς καὶ ἀποκαλύψεως δικαιοκρισίας τοῦ θεοῦ "on *the* day of wrath and of *the* revelation of *the* right judgment of God" (Rom 2,5)

The influence of the Semitic construct chain also explains the absence of the definite article in formulations with the genitive of proper names, including Κύριος (אֲדֹנָי).

ἐν οἴκῳ Δαυὶδ παιδὸς αὐτοῦ "in *the* house of David his son" (Luke 1,69)

ἐκ πόλεως Ναζαρὲθ εἰς τὴν Ἰουδαίαν εἰς πόλιν Δαυίδ "from *the* city of Nazareth into Judea to *the* city of David" (Luke 2,4)

τίς γὰρ ἔγνω νοῦν κυρίου [...] ἡμεῖς δὲ νοῦν Χριστοῦ ἔχομεν "For who knew *the* mind of the Lord [...] but we have *the* mind of Christ" (1 Cor 2,16)

4. USES OF THE PRONOUN

One of the distinctive features of biblical Greek is the frequent use of pronouns to make explicit what is implicitly expressed in the formulation of the sentence. While the same tendency can be observed in the popular style of Hellenistic Greek, the noticeably abundant use of pronouns in the NT can be ascribed to the influence of Semitic usage, where the easy employment of suffix-pronouns favors the heightened use of (pleonastic) pronouns by Greek authors influenced by the Semitic idiom.

4.1. Non-Emphatic Nominative Pronouns

In accordance with good Greek style, the nominative of personal pronouns is used only for emphasis or contrast. Consequently, the *non-emphatic* use of pronouns in the NT suggests Semitic influence.

ἰδοὺ ἐγὼ ἀποστέλλω ὑμᾶς ὡς πρόβατα ἐν μέσῳ λύκων "Behold, I send you like sheep in the midst of wolves" (Matt 10,16)

καὶ ἰδοὺ ἀνὴρ ὀνόματι καλούμενος Ζακχαῖος, καὶ αὐτὸς ἦν ἀρχιτελώνης καὶ αὐτὸς πλούσιος "And behold, [there was] a man named Zachaeus, and he was a chief tax collector and he was rich" (Luke 19,2)

4.2. Pleonastic Pronouns

There are a few instances in the NT where a relative clause has not only the introductory relative pronoun but also a further (pleonastic) pronoun referring to the same antecedent. While extremely rare in literary Greek, added (pleonastic) pronouns are common in Semitic languages, in which the relative particle (Hebrew אֲשֶׁר; Aramaic דִּי) is indeclinable, and so its full determination (gender, number, case) requires an added pronoun in the relative clause that follows.

ἀκούσασα γυνὴ περὶ αὐτοῦ, ἧς εἶχεν τὸ θυγάτριον αὐτῆς πνεῦμα ἀκάθαρτον "A woman, whose daughter (of her) had an unclean spirit, heard about him" (Mark 7,25)

ἔρχεται δὲ ὁ ἰσχυρότερός μου, οὗ οὐκ εἰμὶ ἱκανὸς λῦσαι τὸν ἱμάντα τῶν ὑποδημάτων αὐτοῦ "But he who is mightier than I is coming, whose sandal strap (of him) I am not worthy to untie" (Luke 3,16).

καὶ πάντα τὰ ἔθνη ἐφ' οὓς ἐπικέκληται τὸ ὄνομά μου ἐπ' αὐτούς "And all the Gentiles on whom my name is invoked (on them)" (Acts 15,17; citating the LXX translation of the prophecy in Amos 9,12: וְכָל־הַגּוֹיִם אֲשֶׁר־נִקְרָא שְׁמִי עֲלֵיהֶם)

5. COMPARATIVE AND SUPERLATIVE DEGREES

The fact that the comparative form is lacking in Hebrew and Aramaic explains why in biblical Greek the comparative or superlative is sometimes expressed with the positive form of the adjective. In these instances, the comparative sense of the (positive) adjective can be inferred from the context, such as the use of accompanying constructions with ἤ ("than"), or παρά, ὑπέρ ("beyond"), or ἀπό (cf. Hebrew use of מִן to express comparison).

> καλόν ἐστίν σε εἰσελθεῖν εἰς τὴν ζωὴν χωλὸν ἢ τοὺς δύο πόδας ἔχοντα βληθῆναι εἰς τὴν γέενναν "It is good for you to enter life lame [more] than with two feet to be cast into hell" (Mark 9,45)

> δοκεῖτε ὅτι οἱ Γαλιλαῖοι οὗτοι ἁμαρτωλοὶ παρὰ πάντας τοὺς Γαλιλαίους ἐγένοντο "Do you think that these Galileans were sinners [more] than all the other Galileans?" (Luke 13,2)

> χαρὰ ἐν τῷ οὐρανῷ ἔσται ἐπὶ ἑνὶ ἁμαρτωλῷ μετανοοῦντι ἢ ἐπὶ ἐνενήκοντα ἐννέα δικαίοις "In heaven over one repentant sinner there will be joy [more] than over ninety-nine righteous persons" (Luke 15,7)

Semitic influence is also present in places where the positive degree has a superlative sense in relation to a named group or class.

> εὐλογημένη σὺ ἐν γυναιξίν "most blessed are you among women" (Luke 1,42)

> διδάσκαλε, ποία ἐντολὴ μεγάλη ἐν τῷ νόμῳ; "Teacher, what is the greatest commandment in the Law?" (Matt 22,36)

6. USES OF THE PARTICIPLE

6.1. Periphrastic Conjugation

Greek provides for periphrastic conjugations in which a simple verb form is replaced with a participle and a finite form of the verb εἶναι. While Hellenistic Greek tends to allow for a wider use of periphrastic conjugations, the noticeably high frequency of this phenomenon in the NT strongly suggests the influence of Aramaic, which favors an analogous use of the participle in verbal formulations.

6.2. Pleonastic Participles

Participles are sometimes used in the NT to express an action (often corporal movement or position) that is implicit in the main verb.

> ἀνοίξας τὸ στόμα αὐτοῦ ἐδίδασκεν αὐτούς "having opened his mouth, he was teaching them" (Matt 5,2)
>
> ἐκτείνας τὴν χεῖρα ἥψατο αὐτοῦ "having stretched out his hand, he touched him" (Matt 8,3)
>
> ἀναστὰς ἠκολούθησεν αὐτῷ "having stood up, he followed him" (Mark 2,14)

While there is nothing grammatically unusual in this circumstantial use of the participle, the formulation is considered a Semitism because it imitates a Semitic manner of speech that makes explicit, with a separate verb, an implicit action, which the Greek speaker would normally leave unexpressed. In the Semitic idiom, the two actions are usually expressed with two coordinated finite verbs (linked with a *waw*). The Synoptic Evangelists tend to render this Semitic idiom with a form of subordination that is natural to Greek: the first (implicit) action is expressed with a circumstantial participle, and the second (main) action is expressed with a finite form of the verb. John, in contrast, tends to avoid this subordinate use of the participle, and follows more faithfully the Semitic model with two coordinated finite verbs. This difference is illustrated with the following examples.

Matt 9,7: ἐγερθεὶς ἀπῆλθεν "rising up, he went away"
John 11,29: ἠγέρθη ταχὺ καὶ ἤρχετο "he rose up quickly and went"

Mark 10,49: στὰς ὁ Ἰησοῦς εἶπεν [...] "standing up Jesus said [...]"
John 20,19: ἦλθεν ὁ Ἰησοῦς καὶ ἔστη εἰς τὸ μέσον καὶ λέγει [...] "Jesus came, and stood among them, and said [...]"

Semitic influence also explains the frequent use of the stock formula: ἀποκριθεὶς εἶπεν. The pleonastic nature of the participle in this formulation is especially evident in cases where the speech act is not, in a strict sense, a "response" or an "answer" to anything in the preceding context (see, e.g., Mark 11,14: καὶ ἀποκριθεὶς εἶπεν αὐτῇ [the fig tree]). The expression, ἀποκριθεὶς εἶπεν, represents an imitation of the underlying Semitic formula that is commonly used to introduce direct discourse: וַיַּעַן וַיֹּאמֶר (Hebrew); עָנֵה וְאָמַר (Aramaic). Also in this instance, John tends to follow the Semitic model with two coordinated finite forms, whereas the Synoptic writers render the formula with a subordinated participle and a finite form of the verb.

Matt 3,15: <u>ἀποκριθεὶς</u> δὲ ὁ Ἰησοῦς <u>εἶπεν</u> [...] "Answering, Jesus said [...]"
John 1,48: <u>ἀπεκρίθη</u> Ἰησοῦς <u>καὶ εἶπεν</u> αὐτῷ [...] "Jesus answered and said [...]"

In the NT, finite forms of a verb of saying, asking, answering, and writing are often followed by the participle λέγων or λέγοντες. This imitates a stock formula commonly found in the LXX, in which λέγων or λέγοντες renders the use of the Hebrew infinitive לֵאמֹר (with the sense of "saying") to introduce direct discourse. In the LXX and the NT, this use of λέγων or λέγοντες becomes a fixed expression, whose pleonastic character becomes especially evident when λέγων or λέγοντες is used with a finite form of λέγειν (see, e.g., Luke 7,39: ὁ Φαρισαῖος ὁ καλέσας αὐτὸν εἶπεν ἐν ἑαυτῷ λέγων). Once again, John tends to avoid this pleonastic use of the participle and uses instead a coordinated finite form of λέγειν.

Mark 3,11: <u>ἔκραζον λέγοντες</u> [...] "they cried out saying [...]"
John 12,44: <u>ἔκραξεν καὶ εἶπεν</u> [...] "he cried out and said [...]"

7. USES OF PREPOSITIONS

While Hellenistic Greek generally favors a greater reliance on prepositions for the sake of explicit expression, there are several exceptional prepositional phrases in the NT which can be ascribed to Semitic influence.

7.1. The Preposition εἰς (+ Accusative)

The use of εἰς + accusative in place of a predicate nominative with εἶναι or γίνεσθαι is unusual in Greek, but it corresponds closely to the Hebrew use of לְ to mark the predicate of a nominal sentence.

> ἔσονται οἱ δύο εἰς σάρκα μίαν "The two will become one flesh" (Matt 19,5, citing LXX Gen 2,24)
>
> λίθον ὃν ἀπεδοκίμασαν οἱ οἰκοδομοῦντες, οὗτος ἐγενήθη εἰς κεφαλὴν γωνίας "The stone, which the builders rejected, this one has become the cornerstone" (Matt 21,42, citing LXX Ps 117,22)
>
> καὶ ἔσομαι ὑμῖν εἰς πατέρα καὶ ὑμεῖς ἔσεσθέ μοι εἰς υἱοὺς καὶ θυγατέρας "I will be for you a father, and you will be for me sons and daughters" (2 Cor 6,18, citing loosely LXX 2 Kgdms 7,14)

Similarly, εἰς + accusative is sometimes used in place of a predicate accusative.

> εἰς προφήτην αὐτὸν εἶχον "They held him to be a prophet" (Matt 21,46)
>
> ἤγειρεν τὸν Δαυὶδ αὐτοῖς εἰς βασιλέα "He raised up for them David as king" (Acts 13,22)

7.2. The Preposition ἐν (+ Dative)

In the NT, the preposition ἐν (+ dative) is used in a great variety of ways. Several of these exceptional uses may be attributed to the influence of analogous Semitic constructions with the preposition בְּ. The extensive use of ἐν (+ dative) in an instrumental sense, while not without parallel in Hellenistic Greek, is almost certainly owing to Semitic influence.

> εἰ πατάξομεν ἐν μαχαίρῃ; "Are we to strike with the sword?" (Luke 22,49)

Corresponding Semitic constructions with בְּ may also explain, at least partially, the several instances in which ἐν (+ dative) denotes the manner or attendant circumstances of an action or state of being.

> ἐζήτουν οἱ ἀρχιερεῖς καὶ οἱ γραμματεῖς πῶς αὐτὸν ἐν δόλῳ κρατήσαντες ἀποκτείνωσιν "The chief priests and scribes were seeking how to arrest him by treachery and kill him" (Mark 14,1)

> λέγω ὑμῖν ὅτι ποιήσει τὴν ἐκδίκησιν αὐτῶν ἐν τάχει "I tell you that he will bring about their vindication quickly (lit., in haste)" (Luke 18,8)

> μέλλει κρίνειν τὴν οἰκουμένην ἐν δικαιοσύνῃ "He is going to judge the world in [with] righteousness" (Acts 17,31)

> ἐν ῥάβδῳ ἔλθω πρὸς ὑμᾶς ἢ ἐν ἀγάπῃ; "Shall I come to you with a rod or with love?" (1 Cor 4,21)

The use of ἐν with the dative of the articular infinitive *in a temporal sense* is rare in Greek, but it is very common in the LXX where it renders a Semitic temporal construction with בְּ.

> ἐν τῷ κατηγορεῖσθαι αὐτὸν ὑπὸ τῶν ἀρχιερέων καὶ πρεσβυτέρων οὐδὲν ἀπεκρίνατο "While he was being accused by the chief priests and elders, he made no answer" (Matt 27,12)

ἐγένετο ἐν τῷ σπείρειν ὃ μὲν ἔπεσεν παρὰ τὴν ὁδόν "It happened while he was sowing that some [seed] fell along the road" (Mark 4,4)

ἐν τῷ ὑποστρέφειν αὐτοὺς ὑπέμεινεν Ἰησοῦς ὁ παῖς ἐν Ἰερουσαλήμ "While they were returning, the child Jesus remained in Jerusalem" (Luke 2,43)

7.3. The Use of Adverbs as (Improper) Prepositions

Semitic influence can be seen in the frequent use of certain adverbs as (improper) prepositions:

ἔμπροσθεν / ἐνάντιον / ἐνώπιον (+ genitive) with the sense of "before" or "in the sight of" (cf. לִפְנֵי or בְּעֵינֵי)

ὄπισθεν / ὀπίσω (+ genitive) with the sense of "behind" (cf. אַחֲרֵי)

7.4. Stock Prepositional Phrases

Semitic models stand behind several stock circumlocutions that express, graphically, a prepositional concept. The substantive πρόσωπον is used with ἀπό, παρά, κατά, or πρό to render common Semitic expressions with פָּנִים ("face"): מִפְּנֵי ("from the presence of", "from before"); לִפְנֵי ("in the presence of", "before").

ἀπέστειλεν ἀγγέλους πρὸ προσώπου αὐτοῦ "He sent messengers before him" (Luke 9,52)

οἱ μὲν οὖν ἐπορεύοντο χαίροντες ἀπὸ προσώπου τοῦ συνεδρίου "Then they left the presence of the council, rejoicing" (Acts 5,41)

Forms of χείρ are used with the prepositions ἐν or διά or ἐκ to render common Semitic expressions with יָד ("hand"): בְּיַד ("by the hand of", "by the power/agency of"); מִיַּד ("from the power/rule of").

σωτηρίαν ἐξ ἐχθρῶν ἡμῶν καὶ ἐκ χειρὸς πάντων τῶν μισούντων ἡμᾶς "Salvation from our enemies and from the hand of all who hate us" (Luke 1,71)

διὰ δὲ τῶν χειρῶν τῶν ἀποστόλων ἐγίνετο σημεῖα καὶ τέρατα πολλά "Many signs and wonders were done by the hand of the apostles" (Acts 5,12)

In addition, forms of στόμα are used with the prepositions διά or ἐκ or ἐπί to render common Semitic expressions with פֶּה ("mouth") in connection with divine or human speaking.

οὐκ ἐπ᾽ ἄρτῳ μόνῳ ζήσεται ὁ ἄνθρωπος, ἀλλ᾽ ἐπὶ παντὶ ῥήματι ἐκπορευομένῳ διὰ στόματος θεοῦ "Not by bread alone shall man live, but by every word that proceeds from the mouth of God" (Matt 4,4, citing Deut 8,3)

ἐθαύμαζον ἐπὶ τοῖς λόγοις τῆς χάριτος τοῖς ἐκπορευομένοις ἐκ τοῦ στόματος αὐτοῦ "They marveled at the gracious words that came forth from his mouth" (Luke 4,22)

ἔδει πληρωθῆναι τὴν γραφὴν ἣν προεῖπεν τὸ πνεῦμα τὸ ἅγιον διὰ στόματος Δαυίδ "It was necessary that the scripture be fulfilled which the Holy Spirit had spoken in advance through the mouth of David" (Acts 1,16)

8. SPECIAL USES OF καί

NT Greek is marked by an expanded use of καί as a coordinating conjunction linking two independent clauses (*parataxis*), even in places where the reader would expect some form of subordination (*hypotaxis*). This usage reflects a general tendency in the popular idiom of Hellenistic Greek to move away from the subordination of ideas and the explicit expression of their logical connection. This same tendency, however, was very likely encouraged by the Semitic habit of paratactic expression, in which clauses are linked primarily by the coordinating conjunction *waw*.

8.1. Apodotic καί

In certain instances, a sentence begins with a subordinate clause (temporal, causal, or conditional), and then a καί is inserted to introduce the main clause that follows (the *apodosis*). This usage, unusual in Greek, corresponds to the Hebrew "apodotic *waw*".

> καὶ ὅτε ἐπλήσθησαν ἡμέραι ὀκτὼ τοῦ περιτεμεῖν αὐτὸν, καὶ ἐκλήθη τὸ ὄνομα αὐτοῦ Ἰησοῦς "And when the eight days were completed for him to be circumcised, his name was called Jesus" (Luke 2,21)

> ὡς ἀτενίζοντες ἦσαν εἰς τὸν οὐρανὸν πορευομένου αὐτοῦ, καὶ ἰδοὺ ἄνδρες δύο παρειστήκεισαν αὐτοῖς ἐν ἐσθήσεσι λευκαῖς "When they were gazing into heaven as he went, behold, two men stood by them in white robes" (Acts 1,10)

> ἐάν τις ἀκούσῃ τῆς φωνῆς μου καὶ ἀνοίξῃ τὴν θύραν, καὶ εἰσελεύσομαι πρὸς αὐτὸν καὶ δειπνήσω μετ' αὐτοῦ καὶ αὐτὸς μετ' ἐμοῦ "If anyone hears my voice and opens the door, I will come in to him and eat with him, and he with me" (Rev 3,20)

8.2. Pleonastic καί

The conjunction καί is also used within a formulaic expression taken over from the LXX, which imitates, in a literal way, the Hebrew construction: וַיְהִי... וְ... ("And it happened that ..."). In the LXX, this Semitic formula is rendered: καὶ ἐγένετο + καί + main verb.

> Gen 4,8 (MT): וַיְהִי בִּהְיוֹתָם בַּשָּׂדֶה וַיָּקָם קַיִן אֶל־הֶבֶל אָחִיו וַיַּהַרְגֵהוּ

> Gen 4,8 (LXX): καὶ ἐγένετο ἐν τῷ εἶναι αὐτοὺς ἐν τῷ πεδίῳ καὶ ἀνέστη Καιν ἐπὶ Αβελ τὸν ἀδελφὸν αὐτοῦ καὶ ἀπέκτεινεν

αὐτόν "And it happened that when they were in the plain Cain rose up against Abel and killed him"

The NT use of καὶ ἐγένετο as an introductory formula is especially prominent in Luke-Acts, where the author is deliberately imitating the style of the LXX (39 times in Luke; 19 times in Acts). The main clause that follows is expressed either with a finite form of the verb, or with an infinitive (+ subject accusative). As in the LXX, so also in Luke the formulation often includes a καί at the beginning of the main clause, but not always.

καὶ ἐγένετο ἐν τῇ ἡμέρᾳ τῇ ὀγδόῃ ἦλθον περιτεμεῖν τὸ παιδίον "And it happened on the eighth day that they came to circumcise the child" (Luke 1,59)

ἐγένετο δὲ ἐν μιᾷ τῶν ἡμερῶν καὶ αὐτὸς ἐνέβη εἰς πλοῖον "And it happened on one of the days that he entered into a boat" (Luke 8,22)

9. NEGATION

In Greek, strong negations are usually expressed with forms of οὐδείς, οὐδεῖσα, οὐδέν ("no one", "no thing"). In the NT, however, there are also instances of an alternative construction with forms of πᾶς, πᾶσα, πᾶν + negative particle + verb. This corresponds closely to a common Semitic form of negation: ...כל...לא.

οὐκ ἀδυνατήσει παρὰ τοῦ θεοῦ πᾶν ῥῆμα "Nothing is impossible with God" (Luke 1,37)

ὁ δὲ Πέτρος εἶπεν· μηδαμῶς, κύριε, ὅτι οὐδέποτε ἔφαγον πᾶν κοινὸν καὶ ἀκάθαρτον "And Peter said, 'Never, lord, since I have never eaten anything common or unclean" (Acts 10,14)

CHAPTER TEN
ACCENTUATION OF GREEK WORDS

1. PRELIMINARY DEFINITIONS

1.1. Long and Short Syllables

A Greek word has as many syllables as it has vowels or diphthongs. A syllable containing a long vowel or a diphthong is considered "long," while all others are necessarily considered "short".

Short vowels: α ϵ ι ο υ
Long vowels: ᾱ η ῑ ω ῡ
Diphthongs*: αι ϵι οι υι αυ ϵυ ηυ ου

*Final αι and οι are considered short for purposes of accentuation, except when used in the conjugation of verbs in the optative mood.

1.2. Accented Syllables

Most Greek words have one syllable whose musical pitch varies slightly from that of the other syllables of the word. That syllable is said to be "accented", and this difference in pitch is called the word's "accent".

Acute accent (ά):	marks a raising of the musical pitch
Grave accent (ὰ):	marks a lowering of the musical pitch
Circumflex accent (ᾶ):	marks a raising and lowering of pitch in the same syllable

In the modern pronunciation of ancient Greek, accent is usually shown by an increased stress on the accented syllable rather than by a difference in musical pitch.

1.3. Writing Accents

Accent marks are written over the vowel or diphthong of the syllable to be accented. In the case of a diphthong, the accent stands over the second vowel: e.g., αὐτούς, αὐτοῖς.

When a breathing mark and an accent belong to the same vowel, then the acute or grave accent is written to the right of the breathing mark, while the circumflex is placed just above it: e.g., ἄνθρωπος, ὅλος, οἶκος, ἦν.

When breathing marks and accents belong to capital letters, they retain the same configuration but are placed before the letter: e.g., Ἕλλην, Ἡρῴδης.

2. RULES FOR ACCENTUATION

2.1. General Rules for Greek Accents

No matter how many syllables a word may have, the accent can appear only over one of the last three syllables: the final syllable (the *ultima*, "u"), the second-to-last syllable (the *penult*, "p"), or the third-to-last syllable (the *antepenult*, "a").

2.2. Rules for the *Acute Accent*

Possibilities: appears over ultima, penult, or antepenult
appears over short vowels, long vowels, or diphthongs

Restrictions: CAN appear over the ultima ONLY when a pause follows
(i.e., when followed by a period, comma, or semicolon)

CANNOT appear over the penult when it is accented and contains a long vowel or diphthong and the ultima contains a short vowel
CAN appear over the antepenult ONLY when the ultima contains a short vowel

2.3. Rules for the *Grave Accent*

Possibilities: appears ONLY over the ultima
appears over short vowels or long vowels or diphthongs

Restrictions: MUST replace an acute accent over the ultima when another word directly follows without a pause, and CANNOT appear otherwise

2.4. Rules for the *Circumflex Accent*

Possibilities: appears ONLY over the ultima and the penult
appears ONLY over long vowels or diphthongs

Restrictions: MUST appear over penult when the penult is accented and contains a long vowel or diphthong and the ultima contains a short vowel
CANNOT appear over the penult when the ultima contains a long vowel or diphthong

Summary of the Rules Governing Accentuation

1) a – p – ú + pause
2) a – p – ù + word without a pause
3) a – ṕ – u BUT NOT a – p̄́ – ŭ
4) á – p – ŭ
5) a – p – ū̂
6) a – p̄̂ – ŭ MUST, if -p- is accented, BUT NEVER -p̄̂- if -ū-

2.5. Recessive Accent

The accent of a word is said to be recessive when it goes back from the end of the word as far as allowed by the rules for the possibilities of accent. All finite forms of verbs (i.e., all forms except infinitives and participles) have recessive accent.

Consider: ἔπαυσα, ἐπαύσω, παῦσον, παύσῃ

ἦρξαν, ἤρξατε, ἄρξῃς, ἄρξητε, ἀρξάτω

ἀγγέλλεις, ἀγγέλλετε, ἤγγειλα, ἠγγέλθην, ἠγγείλατε

βούλῃ, βουλέσθω, βούλεσθε, ἐβούλου

2.6. Persistent Accent

The accent of a word is said to be persistent when it tries to stay the same accent, over the same vowel or diphthong, in all the forms of the word unless forced by the rules for the possibilities of accent to change in nature (e.g., from circumflex to acute) or position (e.g., from antepenult to penult). Persistent accents change in nature, exhausting all possibilities for remaining on the same syllable, before changing position. The accent on most nouns and adjectives is persistent and must be learned as part of the vocabulary.

Consider: βιβλίον, βιβλίου

ἄνθρωπος, ἀνθρώπου

νῆσος, νήσου

δρᾶμα, δράματος, δραμάτων

3. EXCEPTIONS TO THE RULES FOR ACCENTUATION

3.1. Exceptions in Recessive Accent

3.1.1. The final diphthong οι in the third person singular of the *Present Optative Active* and αι in the third person singular of the *Aorist Optative Active* count as *long* for the purposes of accentuation.

Consider:		
	παιδεύοιμι	παιδεύοιμεν
	παιδεύοις	παιδεύοιτε
	<u>παιδεύοι</u>	παιδεύοιεν
	παιδεύσαιμι	παιδεύσαιμεν
	παιδεύσαις	παιδεύσαιτε
	<u>παιδεύσαι</u>	παιδεύσαιεν

3.1.2. In the *Aorist Subjunctive Passive*, the accent is *always* a circumflex over the initial vowel of the ending.

Consider:		
	λυθῶ	λυθῶμεν
	λυθῇς	λυθῆτε
	λυθῇ	λυθῶσι(ν)

3.2. Exceptions in Persistent Accent

3.2.1. The diphthongs αι and οι, *when final*, count as short for purposes of accentuation.

Consider: ἄνθρωποι, χῶραι

3.2.2. When nouns of the *First* and *Second Declensions* have an acute accent on the ultima in the nominative singular, the accent is changed to a circumflex in the genitive and dative, singular and plural.

Consider:	ζωή	ζωαί
	ζωῆς	ζωῶν
	ζωῇ	ζωαῖς
	ζωήν	ζωάς
	ἀδελφός	ἀδελφοί
	ἀδελφοῦ	ἀδελφῶν
	ἀδελφῷ	ἀδελφοῖς
	ἀδελφόν	ἀδελφούς

3.2.3. For nouns of the *Third Declension* with *monosyllabic stems*, the accent shifts to the ultima in the genitive and dative, singular and plural; the genitive plural has a circumflex.

Consider:	αἴξ	αἶγες
	αἰγός	αἰγῶν
	αἰγί	αἰξί(ν)
	αἶγα	αἶγας

3.2.4. For *all nouns* of the *First Declension*, the accent in the genitive plural shifts to a circumflex over the ultima.

Consider:	ἡμέρα	ἡμέραι
	ἡμέρας	ἡμερῶν
	ἡμέρᾳ	ἡμέραις
	ἡμέραν	ἡμέρας

Likewise, for all *adjectives* in the *First-and-Third Declension* whose feminine nominative singular ends in short -α- (including Present, Aorist, and Perfect Active Participles), the accent in the genitive plural is always over the ultima, regardless of the accent in the nominative singular.

Consider:

ἡδύς	ἡδεῖα	ἡδύ	ἡδεῖς	ἡδεῖαι	ἡδέα
ἡδέος	ἡδείας	ἡδέος	ἡδέων	ἡδειῶν	ἡδέων
ἡδεῖ	ἡδείᾳ	ἡδεῖ	ἡδέσιν	ἡδείαις	ἡδέσιν
ἡδύν	ἡδεῖαν	ἡδύ	ἡδεῖς	ἡδείας	ἡδέα

λύων	λύουσα	λῦον	λύοντες	λύουσαι	λύοντα
λύοντος	λυούσης	λύοντος	λυόντων	λυουσῶν	λυόντων
λύοντι	λυούσῃ	λύοντι	λύουσιν	λυούσαις	λύουσιν
λύοντα	λύουσαν	λῦον	λύοντας	λυούσας	λύοντα

In contrast, for all *adjectives* in the *First-and-Second Declension* whose feminine nominative singular ends in -η- or -ᾱ- (including the Present Middle/Passive, Aorist Middle, and Perfect Middle/ Passive Participles), the accent *does not* shift to the ultima in the feminine genitive plural.

Consider:

ἄξιος	ἀξία	ἄξιον	ἄξιοι	ἄξιαι	ἄξια
ἀξίου	ἀξίας	ἀξίου	ἀξίων	ἀξίων	ἀξίων
ἀξίῳ	ἀξίᾳ	ἀξίῳ	ἀξίοις	ἀξίαις	ἀξίοις
ἄξιον	ἀξίαν	ἄξιον	ἀξίους	ἀξίας	ἄξια

λυόμενος	λυομένη	λυόμενον	λυόμενοι	λυόμεναι	λυόμενα
λυομένου	λυομένης	λυομένου	λυομένων	λυομένων	λυομένων
λυομένῳ	λυομένῃ	λυομένῳ	λυομένοις	λυομέναις	λυομένοις
λυόμενον	λυομένην	λυόμενον	λυομένους	λυομένας	λυόμενα

3.2.5. In the *Aorist Passive Participles*, the accent is on the penult in all forms except the masculine nominative singular, the neuter nominative and accusative singular, and the feminine genitive plural.

Consider:

λυθείς	λυθεῖσα	λυθέν	λυθέντες	λυθεῖσαι	λυθέντα
λυθέντος	λυθείσης	λυθέντος	λυθέντων	λυθεισῶν	λυθέντων
λυθέντι	λυθείσῃ	λυθέντι	λυθεῖσιν	λυθείσαις	λυθεῖσιν
λυθέντα	λυθεῖσαν	λυθέν	λυθέντας	λυλείσας	λυθέντα

4. PROCLITICS AND ENCLITICS

4.1. Preliminary Definitions

4.1.1. *Proclitics* (προκλίνω, "to lean forward") are words which normally have no accent because then are read so closely with the word that follows.

Examples: certain forms of the definite article: ὁ, ἡ, οἱ, αἱ
the conjunctions εἰ and ὡς
the prepositions εἰς and ἐκ
the negating adverb οὐ - οὐκ - οὐχ

4.1.2. *Enclitics* (ἐγκλίνω, "to lean upon") are words which are so closely attached in pronunciation to the preceding word as to affect, in some cases, the accent of the preceding word.

Examples: the personal pronouns μου, μοι, με, σου, σοι, σε
the particles γε and τε
the indefinite adverbs που, ποτε, πως
all forms of the indefinite pronoun/adjective τις, τι, τινος, τινι, τινα, τινες, τινων, τισι(ν), τινας
the present indicative forms of εἰμι (except the second person singular): εἰμι, ἐστι(ν), ἐσμεν, ἐστε, εἰσι(ν).
the present indicative forms of φημι (except the second person singular): φημι, φησι(ν), φαμεν, φατε, φασι(ν)

Enclitics are either monosyllabic (e) or disyllabic (e–e). In certain instances, disyllabic enclitics have an acute or a circumflex accent on the last syllable (e–é, e–ê)

4.2. Rules for Accentuation

4.2.1. A word ending with an acute accent followed by an enclitic (e, e–e, e–é, e–ê) *does not* change its acute accent to a grave accent; the enclitic does not take any accent:

–a–p–ú + e ἀγαθός τις "some good man"

–a–p–ú + e–e ἀδελφοί τινες "some brothers"

4.2.2. A *monosyllabic* enclitic following a word with an acute accent on the penult has no accent, whereas a *disyllabic* enclitic following a word with an acute accent on the penult does take an accent on its final syllable:

–a–ṕ–u + e λόγῳ τε καὶ ἔργῳ "by word and deed"

–a–ṕ–u + e–é ἀνδράσι τισίν "to some men"

–a–ṕ–u + e–ê ἀνθρώπων τινῶν "of some men"

4.2.3. A word with an acute accent on the antepenult receives from the enclitic an additional acute accent on the ultima; the enclitic does not take any accent:

–á–p–ú + e ἄνθρωποί τε καὶ θεοί "men and gods"

–á–p–ú + e–e ἄνθρωποί τινες "some men"

4.2.4. A word ending with a circumflex keeps its circumflex; the enclitic has no accent:

–a–p–û + e αἱ τιμαὶ τῶν ἀγαθῶν τε καὶ σοφῶν "the honors of the good and wise"

–a–p–û + e–e αἱ τιμαὶ σοφῶν τινων "the honors of some wise men"

4.2.5. A word with a circumflex accent on the penult receives from the enclitic an additional accent on the ultima; the enclitic has no accent:

–a–p̂–ú + e	ἐκεῖνά τε καὶ ταῦτα "those things and these things"
–a– p̂–ú + e–e	δῶρά τινα "some gifts"

4.2.6. In a series of enclitics, each takes an acute accent from the following enclitic; the final enclitic of such a series has no accent:

ἐάν ποτέ τίς τί τινι διδῷ "if anyone ever gives anything to anyone"

4.2.7. A proclitic takes an acute accent when it stands alone at the end of a clause, or when followed by an enclitic; the enclitic has no accent:

ὁ δέ φησιν, οὔ "But he said, 'no'"
εἴ τις "if anyone"

4.2.8. Disyllabic enclitics can retain their accent when: 1) they stand at the beginning of a clause or sentence; or 2) when there is emphasis on the enclitic:

τινὲς μὲν χρυσὸν διδόασιν, τινὲς δ' οὔ "Some give gold, others do not"

5. THE SPECIAL CASE OF ἐστίν

The verbal form ἐστίν becomes ἔστιν, completely losing its character as an enclitic, under certain circumstances:

- when it stands at the beginning of a sentence or clause
- when it signifies existence or possibility
- when it is preceded by οὐκ, μή, ὡς, εἰ, καί, ἀλλά, or τοῦτο
- when it is strongly emphatic

INDEX OF BIBLICAL CITATIONS

Mark

Index of Grammatical Topics

Finito di stampare nel mese di novembre 2018
presso Printbee.it - Noventa Padovana (PD)